Second

Impressions

EDITED BY CLINTON ADAMS

VOLUME SIXTEEN OF THE TAMARIND PAPERS

University of New Mexico Press Albuquerque

SECOND

Second

IMPRESSIONS

Impressions

MODERN

Modern

PRINTS &

Prints &

PRINTMAKERS

Printmakers

RECONSIDERED

Reconsidered

CONTENTS

Introduction and

Acknowledgments

IT IS, I FEAR, ALARMINGLY EASY to make mistakes when writing history, and, once in print, they are very hard to correct. Printed words take on a life of their own and create an illusion of infallibility. All too often, when errors either of omission or commission are recognized, the economics of scholarly publication preclude their correction. This is particularly true in the literature of the modern print, which by comparison with the history of modern painting, sculpture, and architecture finds only a limited audience. Typically, in these circumstances, it is difficult to present new views on topics previously addressed (however inadequately) in the literature, and only slightly less difficult to find a venue for reappraisals that arise from shifts in aesthetic perspective.

This volume of *The Tamarind Papers* serves as a forum for some leading writers in the field, within which they provide second impressions with respect to a variety of topics in late nineteenth- and early twentieth-century printmaking in France, Britain, and the United States.

Pat Gilmour makes use of Paul Signac's unpublished correspondence with his printer Auguste Clot to clarify the circumstances that surrounded publication of his radiant color lithographs in the 1890s. Gabriel P. Weisberg directs attention to the prints of Paul Blanc, an artist whose artistic style and social concerns were at odds with the Modernist spirit of his era; Phillip Dennis Cate further underscores the diversity of late nineteenth-century art in France, reminding us that it included not only the works of Impressionists and Post-Impressionists but also those of some eccentric predecessors of Dada and Surrealism. Nancy E. Green studies the prints of Frank Morley Fletcher, one of the first Western artists to gain an intimate knowledge of Japanese woodcut traditions. First through his work in Britain and later in California, Fletcher visibly influenced the development of the color woodcut in the United States.

A series of articles explores aspects of American printmaking during the first half of the twentieth century. With assistance from Childe Hassam's unpublished writings, I correct some errors in what has been written about his lithographs; Richard Cox and Julie L'Enfant make use of Wanda Gág's long-restricted diaries to interpret the erotic component that underlies her depictions of nature; and Robert P. Conway endeavors to determine the origin of the puzzling "reversed" impressions of Arshile Gorky's lithographs. James Wechsler provides a brief account of the important but little-known accomplishments of the Federal Art Project's lithography unit in San Francisco during the Great Depression. David Acton supplements the catalogue of Will Barnet's graphic work by describing a number of previously unknown prints that have come to the Wor-

cester Art Museum as a gift of the artist; and Sylvan Cole tells us of a "second impression" of John Steuart Curry's familiar lithograph *John Brown*. Charles K. Cuno provides heretofore unavailable information about the life and work of his great uncle, Theodore Cuno, a fine lithographic printer who worked in Philadelphia from 1912 into the 1950s; and Trudy V. Hansen discusses the printmaking archives at Rutgers University and elsewhere, which provide an immense and reliable resource for a history yet to come.

All told, these articles not only add to our knowledge of specific artists and their prints but also suggest methodologies through which other historians may usefully reconsider and reappraise the complex history of the modern print. They are presented with the hope and expectation that other writers will be inspired to address the many intriguing topics that remain to be dealt with and the many revisions and corrections that are yet to be made.

While this volume was in the early stages of preparation, David Acton, Richard S. Field, Pat Gilmour, and Joann Moser provided helpful assistance and suggestions. I am indebted to David Acton, O. J. Rothrock, Linda Tyler, and Gabriel P. Weisberg for subsequent comments on manuscripts considered for inclusion, and to all the authors for the care with which those manuscripts were prepared. I thank the museums and collectors who have graciously given permission to reproduce works in their collections. I also thank Linda Tyler, who with good humor has coordinated the many details associated with publication, and Anne N. Gibbons, who has edited the manuscripts with sensitivity and skill. Kristina E. Kachele has created a handsome design in the best tradition of *The Tamarind Papers*.

CLINTON ADAMS

Second

Impressions

1 | NEW LIGHT ON SIGNAC'S COLOR LITHOGRAPHS—AGAIN!

PAT GILMOUR

THE TITLE OF AN ARTICLE I WROTE for the *Burlington Magazine* of April 1990 promised to throw "new light" on Paul Signac's color lithographs.[1] This new light came partly from a close reading of letters in the archive of the French lithographer Auguste Clot, which proved that several dates in the catalogue raisonné of Signac's prints were inaccurate;[2] and partly from circulating more widely two Signac letters that had surfaced in a British dealer's catalogue: letters that established that the artist's contribution to André Marty's *L'Estampe Originale* was not "originale" at all.[3]

The promised illumination was considerably dimmed, however, if not entirely extinguished, by incorrectly dated illustrations, which neatly canceled out my argument. For although text galleys were sent to me for checking, proofs of the illustrations (several of which were obtained for me by the magazine) were not. Their captions were either written by magazine staff or by the dealers who had lent the images, neither of

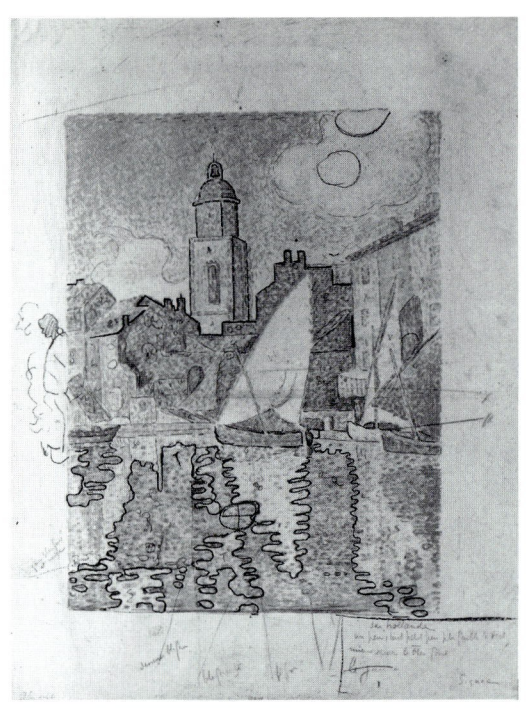

display the rubbed-down mechanical tints that were then the stock-in-trade of the commercial lithographer. Nevertheless, this early example of color lithography made Signac an obvious candidate for André Marty's *L'Estampe Originale*, which included Signac's six-color view of Saint-Tropez in September 1894 (figure 1.2).[5]

Signac's letters, however, reveal that his print for Marty was a reproduction evolved from two of his watercolors, and that it was made at the workshop of Edward Ancourt, chief lithographer to the publication. Either Ancourt or a staff chromiste had two stabs at it—*Saint Tropez I* (KW 5) and *II* (KW 6) —showing the town as a glittering backdrop to an expanse of water, beyond a bank shaded by a large tree.

Signac's response to the printer's first effort was nothing if not brutally frank:

VILLA LA HUNE, 18TH AUGUST 1894
It is a disaster: inexperienced with litho, far away from the printshop, deprived of the rough attraction of the stones, I made [something] horrific: it was so grievous, that it is impossible for us to let it appear. Moreover, they have not done as I asked: in place of the dirty wishy-washy yellow placed on the houses, I had indicated a very intense buttercup yellow—gaudy, dashing, sunny. This goose-shit doesn't give the right effect at all. . . . It is wan and feeble. The contrast, shade against a backdrop of the vile sun, as J.-K. Huysmans put it, completely misfires. The sky, which I wanted blue, rose, orange-colored and white; the foreground lacking in gradation: the red rim of the idiotic boat, etc. Only some parts of the tree are fit to be looked at (assuming they give me my yellow-orange in place of the excremental tint employed). Even so, I had sent a water-

whom seemed to have read my text. To crown everything, the illustration of *Saint-Tropez: Le Port* (KW19) (figure 38 in *Burlington*) was erroneously dated 1894 and was related to that part of my text discussing Signac's contribution to *L'Estampe Originale* (KW 6). In fact, it was a fascinating annotated proof belonging to the National Gallery of Victoria, which shows a different view of the town and was made for Vollard in 1898 (figure 1.1). Following my strangled cry of pain, a minuscule correction was buried in a bushel of announcements at the back of the next issue.

Signac made a dozen color lithographs in all. The first appeared in 1888–89, well before the full flowering of color lithography, on a Théâtre Libre program featuring the chromatic circle of the color theorist, Charles Henry.[4] If the hand-dotted images of countless chromolithographers are discounted, it is the first example of Pointillism in graphic art. Hand-drawn with random dotting and a kind of plus-and-minus notation, the capital *T* and *L*

color to Edward. It is neither what I did, nor what I wanted to do, and contrary to what I feel. I think it best if I postpone it to the next number, or if your prefer it, that I send you a water-color to be reproduced exactly. If I was in Paris, I would touch up the stones and endeavor to save them—but from here?? Pretty tedious for both of us. Very cordially, Signac.

(PS) I attach a little design: if it were possible to achieve this by rubbing the white sail with yellow, changing the yellow on the houses, flooding the background with deep blue, and graduating the sky (blue, orange, rose and violet) with the brush, this could still work.[6]

A second letter, sent just before publication in September, makes it clear that Marty had the print redrawn, for Signac states that he has received and returned a proof indicating a few simple retouches and that he sent back the edition the morning after receiving the printed sheets.[7] It is equally clear that although he was contributing to a series entitled "The Original Print"—and it had long been established that "originality" required artists to draw their own matrices—Signac did not go to Paris.

When André Mellerio pontificated about originality in his short but influential book of 1898, he needed only to perceive the merest whiff of a reproduction or facsimile to seek out and destroy it.[8] Rodin's brilliantly translated watercolors were damned; Cézanne was criticized for allowing Auguste Clot to color his large monochrome print of bathers; while Sisley, despite the fact that he was dying of cancer, was taken to task for not producing *Les Bords de Rivière* (Les Oies) unaided. Yet Signac and Redon, whose pastel of *Béatrice* had been interpreted as a lithograph by Clot, escaped rebuke.[9] Castigation for lack of "orig-

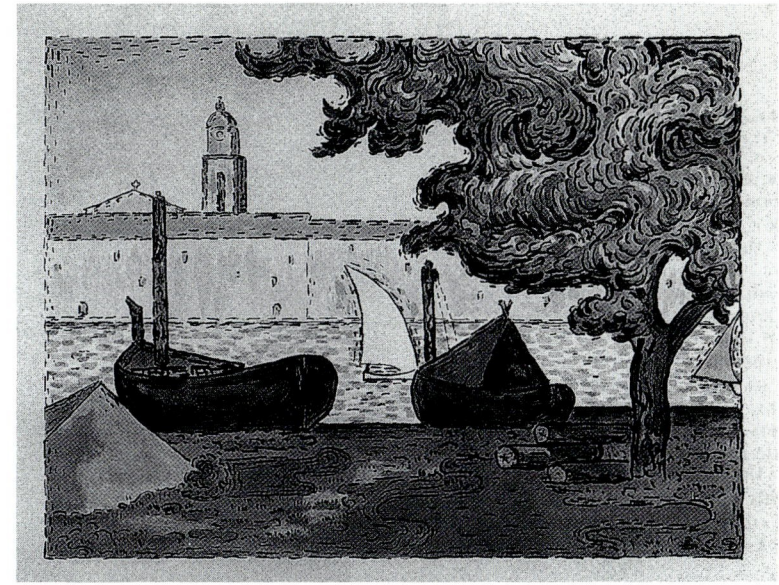

1.2 PAUL SIGNAC. *Saint-Tropez II* (KW 6). Six-color lithograph, 27.4 x 36.8 cm. Drawn and printed at the workshop of Edward Ancourt, and published in *L'Estampe Originale,* Fascicule 7, July-September 1894.

inality" thus depended not so much upon how one's print was actually made as upon whether the printer's assistance was detected at the time.

The dates of Signac's views of Saint-Tropez are well attested, but those traditionally given to his six lithographs for Gustave Pellet are several years too early. The print catalogue raisonné and the memorial catalogue for the publishing house (run after Pellet's death by his son-in-law, Maurice Exsteens),[10] both published by Kornfeld, date *En Hollande—La Balise* and *La Bouée* (KW 8, 9) to 1894, and *Les Andelys* (figure 1.3), *A Flessingue, Les Bateaux à Flessingue,* and *Les Bateaux* (KW 10–13) to 1895. Yet all six prints were proofed and editioned by Clot, for whose independent practice there is no evidence before 1896.[11] Nor is the catalogue raisonné internally consistent, since it gives dates for prints at odds with the dates of drawings and printings on which they are said to be based. *La Bouée,* for example, comes directly from *La Bouée Rouge: Vue de Saint-Tropez,* which bears the date "95" in the lower right corner and was first exhibited early in 1896. The

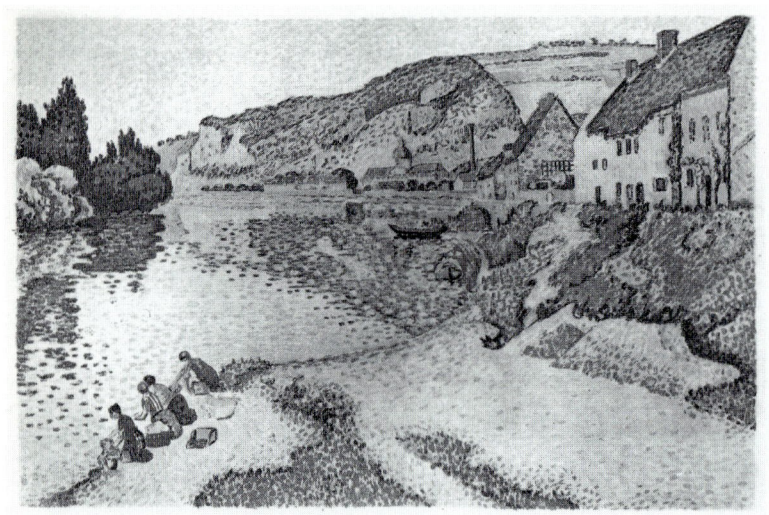

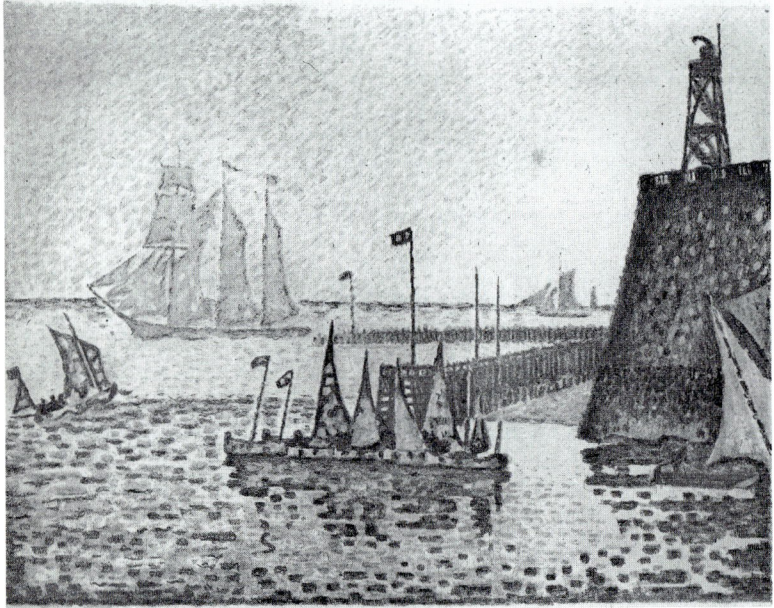

1.3 PAUL SIGNAC. *Les Andelys* (KW 10), 1897 (?). Seven-color lithograph, 30.3 x 45.3 cm. Printed by Auguste Clot and published by Gustave Pellet.

1.4 PAUL SIGNAC. *Abend (Soir)* (KW 20). Five-color lithograph, 20.2 x 26.1 cm. Printed by Auguste Clot and published in *Pan,* vol. 4, 1898.

and since Wick is credited as its joint author, it is difficult to understand why these dates were not corrected.[13]

Signac's connection with Clot is documented by seven surviving cards or letters, the appearance of ten annotated or dedicated proofs in the printer's sale of 1919;[14] and by thirty-eight unspecified color prints and three unnamed *originaux* that remained in the estate at Mme Clot's death in 1954.[15] The numerous variant color proofs with detailed inscriptions for amendment, or *bon-à-tirer* impressions allowing editioning only *après les corrections indiquées,* suggest that although Signac took a more direct interest in his prints after the experience with *L'Estampe Originale,* he continued to leave a good deal of retouching to his printer.[16]

The letters sent to August Clot by Signac confirm that at least one of the Pellet images must be redated to 1898, for they establish that an unnamed print for Pellet and the high-key, sunlit marine of Saint-Tropez intended for Vollard's third, unrealized, album of 1898 (KW 19) were produced either synchronously or slightly later than the lithograph *Abend (Soir)* (KW 20) (figure 1.4), which came out in July 1898 in the German luxury magazine *Pan.*

The *Pan* commission involved an article and a lithograph by Signac, and lithographs by his friend Henri-Edmond Cross and two other Neo-Impressionist associates, Maximilien Luce and Hippolyte Petitjean; the date work began is established by excerpts from Signac's published journals.[17] On 29 December 1897, Signac records that "a young German collector . . . in love with color and light" has asked him, and other Pointillists, to make a set of lithographs for *Pan.* This pinpoints to a very late December 1897 or early January 1898 an undated note to Clot that asks the printer to estimate by return

prints of Flessingue (the Dutch port also known as Flushing or Vlissingen) are also based on paintings of 1896. And not only did Signac's first visit to Holland take place in 1896, but an entry in one of his unpublished journals discusses a trial for the lithograph *La Bouée* on 15 April 1897.[12] Indeed, the date of 1897–98 for the Pellet prints was established in an essay by Peter Wick twelve years before the catalogue raisonné was published,

courier how much it will cost to edition "three lithographs each 20 x 26 [cm] in five colors—on average—in an edition of 1,237 (1,100 ordinary and 137 on Japon)." Clot is begged to "make the price as reasonable as possible; it's for a high quality, prestigious journal that it is in your interest to please."[18]

Signac's journal goes on to reveal that he and the German, Count Kessler, visited various dealers and studios in Paris together and that Signac read to Kessler from a manuscript he was then writing about Delacroix and color theory. Part of this, under the title "Neoimpressionismus," also appeared in the German magazine.

On his return to Germany, Kessler wired Signac that he had received approval to commission the prints, whereupon Signac sent Clot another short note, quoting the telegram, and telling him to "go right ahead."[19] A third, undated note from Signac's Paris address announces that Cross and Signac are coming to see Clot about their plates, "which are finished except for any modifications you may suggest to us."[20] Although Cross made an earlier lithograph with Clot, published by Vollard in 1897, the *Pan* prints provide the most likely reason for the artists to visit Clot's workshop together.

The only dated letter from Signac to Clot was written in Auteuil on 16 April 1898 (figure 1.5). In it Signac expresses sympathy to Clot for his "recent loss" and hopes that "a little happiness soon returns to your so distressing life."[21] While the letter is not specific, the printer is known to have lost a child, and he and his wife received similar condolences from others. If the child had been ill for a while, this family tragedy might explain Clot's tardiness and Signac's considerable annoyance:

Having had confidence in your promise to deliver proofs to us on Tuesday, I promised M. de Kessler that I'd send them to him at the same time as I sent him an article he'd asked me to write. Not having received anything from you, I sent the article off without the proofs. And M. de Kessler is very annoyed. He has been waiting for two months now. It is *absolutely in your own interest* to do this immediately. Put everything else aside, because this is more urgent.

I'm at my wits end with all these delays and I beg you to fix a guaranteed completion date right now for the Vollard and Pellet plates. I'll be paying on the 15th and I need to be able to retouch my stones. You know that I'm both serious and punctual and if I have to go off without having seen those proofs I shall be very annoyed. I've waited my turn long enough. So I ask you this instant to set a date when the Vollard proof will be ready and to do immediately what you have to do to have the Pellet plate transferred to stone and to pull the proofs. Don't give me the excuse that Pellet is not in a hurry. I am, and if he doesn't want the plate, then I'll publish it at my expense.
Regards, P. Signac.[22]

It is this letter chiding Clot that proves that Signac's only lithograph for Vollard and at least one of the images for Pellet were in the workshop at the same time as the 1898 print for *Pan*. Although the letter bears no date, Signac's statement that Kessler has waited "two months," his complaint that he may have to "go off without seeing these proofs," and the fact that he has had to send his article to Kessler without the lithograph, all point to mid-March 1898. The artist's diary mentions finishing his manuscript on 7 March, while

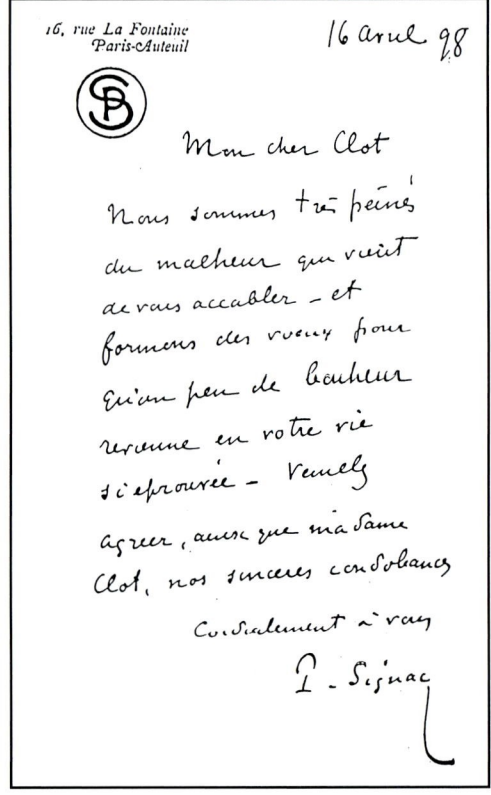

day Signac left the south of France to winter
in Paris, reads:

> My dear Clot,
> We're leaving for Paris today. Could
> you kindly have the *Pan*, Vollard and
> Pellet proofs ready for me so that I can
> pick them up the moment I arrive. My
> regards to Madame Clot.
> Yours, P. Signac.[24]

Signac's diary for 13 December 1898 speaks
of a "sad awakening" in Paris, desolate under
rain, after the beautiful golden light of Saint-
Tropez, and dates his last extant communication to Clot around 11 December. When
Signac's journal for 1896–97 is published it
will substantiate that most of Pellet's lithographs belong to the latter part of this period,
while the letters to Auguste Clot conclusively
prove that at least one of the six was not
completed until 1898.

the placing of the print commission in January upon receipt of Kessler's telegram is
also consistent with a two-month wait. As
to Signac's imminent departure, on 11 March
his diary refers to a forthcoming "Turner pilgrimage," and a separate notebook, enthus-
ing about Turner's magic, reveals that he left
for London on 27 March. His April letter of
sympathy to Clot confirms his return to the
French capital.

In a short note from his Saint-Tropez studio, to which he traveled around 16 August,
Signac asks what has happened to *Pan*, and
requests Clot either to send or set aside for
him the artist's proofs to which he is entitled.[23]
The diary reveals that it was 18 October before Signac saw the July issue of the publication featuring his work, and the only remaining communication to Clot, a card written the

Notes

*All Signac's letters were written in French, and are
accented exactly as written; translations are by Pat
Gilmour and Mark Henshaw.*

1. Pat Gilmour, "New Light on Signac's Colour
   Lithographs," *Burlington Magazine* (April 1990):
   271–75.
2. E. W. Kornfeld and P. A. Wick, *Catalogue Raisonné
   de l'Oeuvre Gravé et Lithographié de Paul Signac*
   (Berne: Editions Kornfeld and Klipstein, 1974),
   cited throughout as KW.
3. Warrack and Perkins Catalogue, Oxford, Summer
   1987; list 36, item 31: "Paul Signac—two auto-
   graph letters signed, to the director of 'L'Estampe
   Originale,' André Marty, 18 August 1894 and
   lundi matin (September 1894), from Villa La
   Hune, St. Tropez, 6pp in all, oblong 8vo.
   £250,000." The text of both these "important

and revealing letters" is published, together with the cataloguer's theories as to their implications.

4. *Application du Cercle Chromatique de Mr. Ch. Henry, 1888,* color lithograph, 15.5 x 18 cm, printed by Eugène Verneau (KW 4).

5. See no. 69, fascicule 7 in Donna Stein, *L'Estampe Originale* (New York, 1970).

6. VILLA LA HUNE, 18 AOÛT, 1894

C'est un désastre: inexperimenté en litho, éloigné de l'imprimerie, privé du rude charme des pierres, j'ai fait une horreur: c'était presque fatal, qu'il nous est impossible de laisser paraître. On n'a du reste pas fait ce que j'ai demandé: à la place du sale ton pisseux jaune mis sur les maisons, j'avais indiqué un jaune très intense, bouton d'or, gueulard, hurleur, soleilleux. Cette merde d'oie ne rend pas du tout l'effet . . . C'est incolore, et mou. L'effet, contraste d'ombre sur fond de soleil crapuleux, comme dirait J.-K. Huysmans, est complètement raté. Le ciel que je voulais bleu, rose, orangé et blanc; le premier plan manque de dégradé: le liston rouge du bâteau imbécile, etc. Seules quelques parties de l'arbre peuvent être regardées (en admettant que l'on me rende mon jaune orangé au lieu de l'excrementielle teinte employée). J'avais pourtant envoyé une aquarelle à Edward [Ancourt]. Ce n'est ni ce que j'ai fait ni ce que j'ai voulu faire, et le contraire de ce que je sens. Je pense que le mieux est de me remettre au prochain numéro ou bien voulez-vous que je vous adresse une aquarelle que l'on ferait reproduire exactement. Si j'étais à Paris je maquillerais les cailloux et tâcherais de les sauver—mai d'ici?? Bien ennuyé pour nous deux et bien cordialement. Signac.

(PS) Ci-joint un petit modèle: si l'on pourrait arriver à ceci en frottant de jaune la voile blanche, échangeant en jaune les maisons, en noyant dans un bleu foncé tout le plan, et en faisant un dégradé de ciel (bleu, orangé, rose, violet) à la brosse, cela irait encore.

7. The letter, dated "lundi matin" (September 1894) reads:

J'ai trouvé l'épreuve fort réussie sauf de facils retouches et je vous remercie de vos excellents soins—Voulez-vous me faire parvenir 2 ou 3 épreuves définitives—j'ai renvoyé l'épreuve corrigée *une* heure après sa reception et les feuilles

signées, récues hier soir 5 heures ont eté expédiées ce matin à la première heure. . . .

Warrack and Perkins's cataloguer suggests that Signac presigned sheets of paper, but I am inclined to think that Signac expressed himself awkwardly, because two separate operations were clearly involved—the making of the corrections and subsequently the return of the corrected edition, which he presumably signed overnight.

8. André Mellerio, La Lithographie en Couleurs (Paris, 1898), trans. Margaret Needham, in Phillip Dennis Cate and Sinclair H. Hitchings, *The Color Revolution: Color Lithography in France, 1890–1900* (Santa Barbara: Peregrine Smith, 1978).

9. See my essay "Cher Monsieur Clot," in *Lasting Impressions: Lithography as Art* (Canberra: Australian National Gallery, 1988). Redon's *Béatrice* is discussed on p. 162 n. 107. Since this book appeared, the Redon pastel, from the collection of Gisèle Rueff-Béghin, has changed hands at Sotheby's London in the sale of *Impressionists and Modern Paintings and Drawings,* 19 November 1988, cat. 16. The pastel is virtually identical to multicolor proofs of *Béatrice* showing flickering lights and flowers behind the subject's head. The edition, eventually supervised and edited by the artist, is based on the unadorned form of the head, as drawn by Clot, with a spray of laurel leaves added top right.

10. *La Maison Gustave Pellet—Maurice Exsteens,* catalogue 106, Berne (24 May 1962).

11. Clot and his descendants kept some eight hundred letters sent to him at his workshop. Copies of these letters have been made available to me by Dr. Guy Georges, grandson of Auguste Clot; except as otherwise noted, all Signac letters are from this source and are quoted by Dr. Georges's kind permission. The earliest surviving letter, from Jacques-Emile Blanche, is dated 2 April 1896. Before that, Clot worked for the great Parisian printer, Lemercier, to whom he was apprenticed at eleven or twelve years of age.

12. Information from Marina Ferretti, who is working with Françoise Cachin on the catalogue raisonné of the artist's paintings. Ferretti also advises that Signac's as yet unpublished journal for 1896–97 records visits to Clot's atelier on 11 and 28 December 1896 and 18 and 25 January, 6

February, 28 March, 11 and 15 April, and 1 May 1897 (Ferrettti to Gilmour, 14 September and 9 October 1989). Published excerpts from the journal (see n. 17 below) reveal another visit made in 1897. The entry for 12 April 1897 reads: "At the printer's I met [Maurice] Denis who interviewed me quite a bit on division—I think that this roublard [old fox] would like to pilfer its advantages." Denis made several images with Clot in 1897.

13. Peter A. Wick, "Some Drawings Related to Signac's Prints," in *Prints*, ed. Carl Zigrosser (New York: Holt, Rinehart and Winston, 1962), 83–96. I have tried, but failed, to trace Peter Wick.

14. See *Catalogue des lithographies de . . . composant la collection de M. A. C.*, Hôtel Drouot, salle no. 7, Paris, 13 June 1919. The Signac entry on pp. 22 and 24 is as follows (I have added in brackets currently accepted titles or my best estimate of present-day identities):

Signac (Paul)

158. *Les Blanchisseuses.* Deux épreuves d'essai, imp. en couleurs, une avec de nombreuses annotations manuscrites [*Les Andeleys*, KW 10].

159. *Marine: plein soleil.* Deux épreuves, imp. en couleurs, une avec annotations, la 2e avec dédicace, signée [several possibilities].

160. La même estampe. Très belle épreuve, imp. en couleurs, avec remarque.

161. *Plein soleil.* Deux épreuves, imp. en couleurs, une retouchée au crayon et annotée, la 2e avec dédicace [*Saint-Tropez—Le Port*, KW 19].

162. *Brume.* Très belle épreuve, imp. en couleurs, avec dédicace [*En Hollande* (?) KW 8].

163. *Les Barques à voiles.* Très belle épreuve d'essai, imp. en couleurs [*La Bouée*, KW 9].

164. *Récréation au bord de la mer.* Très belle épreuve, imp. en couleurs, dédicace [KW 14].

15. From the listing of Clot's estate, handled by the Paris dealer, Paul Prouté.

16. In an essay on Toulouse-Lautrec, Antony Griffiths suggests that the artist had stones "corrected or even drawn" by the printer, and adds that "this certainly is the implication of various annotations found on trial proofs." See "The Prints of Toulouse-Lautrec," in *Toulouse-Lautrec: The Complete Prints*, Wolfgang Wittrock (London: Sotheby, 1985), 41.

17. See "Extraits du Journal inédit de Paul Signac" (Part 1: 1894–95; 2: 1897–98; 3: 1898–99), in *Gazette des Beaux-Arts,* part 1 (July-September 1949): 97–128, 166–74; 2 (April 1952): 265–84, 298–304; 3 (July-August 1953): 27–57, 72–80. The paired page numbers refer to French originals followed by English translations.

18. 16, rue La Fontaine / Paris-Auteuil / [PS monogram]
Mon cher Clot,

1. Tous mes souhaits pour vous et votre famille.

2. Combien couterait le tirage—tout compris—de 3 lithos de 20 sur 26 de cinq couleurs—en moyenne—tiré à 1237 (1100 ordinaires et 137 Japon)—chacune.

Faites le prix le plus modéré; c'est pour un journal allemand riche et sérieux auquel vous auriez intérêt à plaire.

3. Répondez-moi par retour du courrier—on attend votre réponse.

4. Je vous serre la main.
P. Signac.

19. [Auteuil address and monogram] Dimanche
Cher Clot,

Reçu hier soir cette dépeche: Adhesion obtenue avances seront enyoyees Kessler. Vous pouvez donc y aller carrement.
A vous. P. Signac.
Compliments a Mme Clot.

20. [card] Dimanche
Mon cher Clot,

Nous irons Cross et moi vous consulter demain après midi (Lundi) sur nos planches, qui sont terminées, sauf les modifications que vous nos indiquerez.
Cordialement. P. Signac.

21. [Auteuil address and monogram] 16 Avril '98
Mon cher Clot,

Nous sommes très peinés du malheur qui vient de vous accabler—et formons des voeux pour qu'un peu de bonheur revienne en votre vie si éprouvée. Veuillez agréer aussi que Madame Clot, nos sincères condoléances.
Cordialement à vous. P. Signac.

22. [Auteuil address and monogram]

Confiant en votre promesse de nous livrer les épreuves Mardi, j'avais promis à M. de Kessler de les lui envoyer en même temps que le manuscrit d'un article qu'il m'a commandé. N'ayant rien reçu de votre part, j'ai du envoyer l'article sans les épreuves. Et M. de Kessler est fort mécontent. Voici deux mois qu'il attend. Il est *absolument de votre intérêt* de faire immédiatement cet essai. Remettez tout autre travail, car celui là est plus qu'urgent.

Je suis effrayé de tous ces délais et je vous prie de fixer dès à présent, comme je vous l'ai demandé, une date certaine pour l'essai de la planche Vollard et de la planche Pellet. Je pais le 15 et il faut que je puisse retoucher mes pierres. Vous savez que je suis sérieux et exact et si je devais m'en aller sans avoir vu ces essais je serais fort mécontent. Il y a longtemps que j'ai retenu mon tour. Je vous prie donc de me fixer dès à présent un rendevous pour l'essai du Vollard et de prendre vos précautions pour qu'immédiatement vous reportiez sur pierre la planche Pellet et en fassiez les essais. Ne me donnez pas comme raison que Pellet n'est pas pressé. Moi, je le suis et s'il ne veut pas de cette planche je l'éditerai à mon compte. Je vous serre la main. P. Signac.

23. [The printed address "15 rue Hégésippe Moreau" has been crossed out and "S Tropez Var" substituted]
Mon cher Clot,

Où en est le tirage du Pan? Dites un peu. Envoyez moi ou conservez moi, je vous prie, les épreuves auxquelles nous devons avoir droit. Mes meilleurs compliments à Madame Clot. Bien à vous. P. Signac.

24. [card]
Mon cher Clot,

Nous partons aujourd'hui pour Paris.

Vous serez bien aimable de me préparer mes épreuves du Pan, de Vollard, et de Pellet que j'irai prendre dès mon arrivée.

Mes compliments à Mme Clot.

Bien à vous. P. Signac.

2 | PAUL BLANC'S

Mendicity as

BEGGARS

Metaphor

GABRIEL P. WEISBERG

IN THE LATE NINETEENTH CENTURY, few artists focused with such purpose on the theme of misery as did Paul Blanc (1836–1910), a long-neglected printmaker from the south of France, whose works were occasionally included in Parisian Salons or in private exhibitions during the 1880s and 1890s.[1]

Blanc was not yet twenty when his family sent him to study art in Paris, where in 1856–57 he worked in the studio of Charles Gleyre, met several leading academic painters, gained the confidence of Meissonier, and later studied with Jean-Léon Gérôme.[2] By the mid-1860s, he was a student at the Ecole des Beaux-Arts, where he forged friendships with Henri Regnault and Alexandre Rapin.[3] During these formative years, Blanc developed an interest in themes of lower-class life that would lead him throughout his career to create numerous drawings and prints of beggars.

In 1867, when his father sustained an injury, Blanc cut short his study in Paris and returned home to La Verdière, a mountain village north and east of Aix-en-Provence.

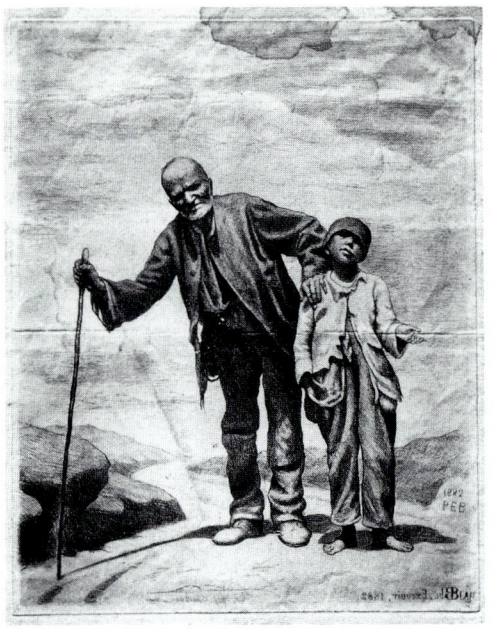

His father wanted him to pursue a practical career as a doctor, but through the intervention of family members, young Blanc was sent to Italy in 1868, where he could study the old masters and complete religious paintings for provincial churches. After a brief period of independence, Blanc returned home for a few years (1869–73) before he began the life of a wanderer and itinerant artist (1873–83).[4] During these ten years he produced paintings—including *Mendiants* (figure 2.1), which was accepted by the 1882 Salon on the recommendation of Alfred Roll—that drew on his association with beggars.[5] Exhausted by years of travel and encouraged by his growing visibility in Paris, Blanc developed images of beggars based upon both personal experience and familiarity with the work of other artists who depicted them, such as Jacques Callot and Rembrandt. A strong penchant existed among nineteenth-century artists to transform the beggar into an icon that would represent the destitute condition of many members of society.[6] Blanc had little difficulty finding models: beggars stood on

street corners in large cities and they traveled the roads of the countryside. For some, begging became a way of life; for Blanc, it became a metaphor for the human condition and a theme that would dominate his career.[7]

His obsession with this theme led him to compose a treatise that offers a detailed iconographic reading of various types of beggars.[8] This unpublished treatise, in Blanc's handwriting, suggests that the artist prepared and modified the text over a long period. It functions as an intimate journal that provides insight into the ways Blanc visualized beggars and records how earlier writers and artists described them .

BLANC'S CATEGORIES OF BEGGARS

In his astute treatise on beggars, Blanc carefully separated them as individuals and as members of groups that could be easily identified and sorted into categories, eight for men and three for women.[9] Blanc's own drawings and etchings of beggars frequently conform to the ways he wrote about them in his text, and often images can be linked to specific passages. Undoubtedly, Blanc did much preparatory work, consulting earlier writings about beggars in order to place his work within a larger social context (figures 2.2 and 2.3).

Blanc's careful categorization of the lower classes of society indicates that his overall view of humanity, though bleak, was not pessimistic: he was simply thorough, obsessed, and nonjudgmental. He developed an almost romantic vision of beggars as free spirits and seems to have been fascinated by their picturesque nature. Indeed, he had lived and traveled with them when he journeyed through Italy as a young man.

14

Gabriel P. Weisberg

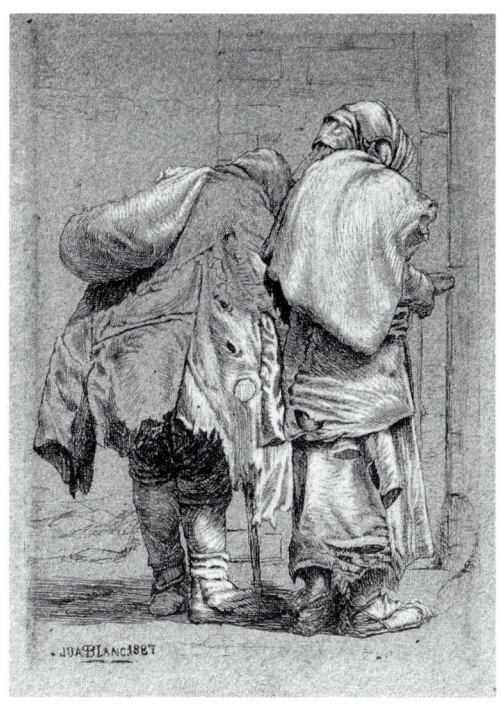

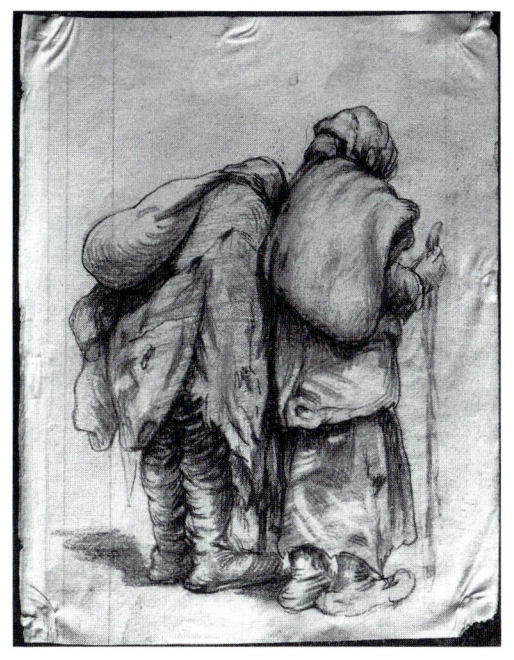

Throughout his detailed treatise Blanc tried to decipher the complex nature of the beggar in society. He categorized beggars according to types and conditions; he identified their characteristics and habits, and the tricks

they used to swindle generous souls; and he carried over this precise categorization into his examination of female vagabonds. The distinct possibility emerges that Blanc sought to use beggars as a metaphor for society itself. The presence of beggars could demonstrate that society was crumbling and that mankind existed in a state of decadence. The average person, like the beggar, lived in a state of constant despair. Since Blanc's prints and drawings were exhibited principally during the 1890s, when the theme of decadence and the decline of Western society appeared in many writings, it is likely that Blanc's prints, when they were noticed, were equated with the general decay of life.[10] If so, this could further account for the public and critical interest that was then expressed in Blanc's imagery.

In advancing this theory about the significance of Blanc's beggars, one must ask if his use of the theme was unique and if he developed his theoretical concepts and categories with some degree of assistance from other written texts. Admittedly, the depiction of beggars had long been a part of the visual arts in the nineteenth century and before. Blanc's overarching commitment to the theme of the vagabond or the wanderer brought with it an interest in earlier artists who had incorporated that theme in their work.

THE WRITTEN SOURCES OF BLANC'S BEGGARS

By the 1890s, an array of publications on the history and significance of beggars existed. Blanc, with his training at the Ecole des Beaux-Arts and his strong humanistic background, most likely read many of them. The information he derived from such sources would have supported the need to divide

2.2 PAUL BLANC. *Perseverance* (Catalogue Paul Blanc 34; Blanc/Ripert 31), 1887. Drypoint, 16.5 x 11.5 cm. Private collection.

2.3 PAUL BLANC. *Perseverance,* ca. 1887. Charcoal, 17.5 x 12.5 cm. Private collection.

beggars into groups and would have helped Blanc to delineate the beggar community.

While the history of beggars is not the focus of this article, it is important to recall that in their long history their treatment changed over time. When Blanc created his images, many Western countries published books that recorded the lives, appearances, and habits of beggars. Other treatises discussed how this segment of the population should be handled, treated, and controlled.[11] Exposés were legion, and endless popular novels attesting to the plight of beggars appeared in the sixteenth, seventeenth, and eighteenth centuries.[12]

During the Second Empire, the period during which Blanc became addicted to the theme, beggars were increasingly seen as hardened criminals or as mentally ill, hence they constituted a segment of society that was deemed to be extremely dangerous. Social conditions for beggars took another turn for the worse in the 1890s, when their population grew so much that they overran the countryside, intimidating farmers who refused them assistance. The penal code divided vagabonds into distinct groups: those who could not work due to handicaps; those who were unemployed for reasons beyond their control; and those who did not want to work: the professional beggars.[13] Public assistance cared for the first and second groups; the penal system handled the third group, which had become the dominant category. This toughened policy served to balance growing tension and heightened public concern about beggars. Numerous government authorities sought to increase assistance to the poor and to add to the number of shelters provided for the homeless. Nevertheless, by the 1880s it had become apparent that the government had failed to eliminate pauperism. Thus, Blanc's drawings and prints of the

next decade underscored that the problems associated with vagabonds were anything but resolved.

While it is unclear which country—Italy or France—inspired Blanc to pursue the theme of beggars, conditions were apparently the same throughout Europe. The rise of this lowest of classes was endemic to the age. In a sense then, Blanc had seized upon a theme that was both personal and pan-European.

Blanc was well aware of the work of Rembrandt, who had explored the theme of beggars early in his own career. In the seventeenth century Rembrandt responded to the increased sense of humanity and compassion for beggars, who came to be seen less as rogues than as tragic figures.[14] In a number of his prints Rembrandt studied the despair and wretchedness that surrounded beggars. Instead of blaming them for their poverty, Rembrandt found tragedy in their shabby clothing and unsteady gait, as if their spirit had been crushed by impersonal forces beyond their control.[15] Such heightened compassion was instigated by the new moral imperatives of the Reformation, which caused people to believe that they had a moral obligation to help the less fortunate. The social consciousness of seventeenth-century Holland formed a new way to think about beggars, which allowed people to be emotionally moved by the poor and inspired action to eliminate poverty.[16]

As models for Blanc's own etchings, Rembrandt's prints (figure 2.4) confronted the notion of shabbiness and forced the viewer to confront the diseases that afflicted the poor.[17] In focusing on those at the lowest level of society, these two artists noted the parallel between mankind and the beggar. They helped create a visual symbol that followed the precept of "on earth we are all beggars, as Christ himself was."[18] Instead of seeing a vagabond as a vile figure bereft of redeeming qualities, Blanc promoted the belief that the beggar was a noble individual, whose low position in society embodied a type of innate humility. This attitude reflected certain preachings of the nineteenth century.

> The wisdom of God is not according to the wisdom of the world. . . . [Christ came] not in riches and great pomp, but in poverty and in rags; . . . his disciples, . . . the vilest men on the world; as St. Paul saith, "excrementa mundi," "outcasts of the world." And so shall all his disciples be, all they that will be saved by him . . . will you have Christ? Where shall you find him? Not in the jollities of the world, but in rags, in the poor people. Have you any poor people amongst you in your town and city? Seek him there amongst the rags. There you shall find him.[19]

Seeking Christ amongst the rags is exactly what Rembrandt did in his numerous prints of vagabonds. Since Blanc astutely observed Rembrandt's etchings and left texts discussing his thoughts on the Dutch artist's work, it is easy to conclude that he shared the same point of view.[20] Blanc's own etchings create a spiritual effect, and his use of chiaroscuro and dark environments creates a sense of mystery that suggests an intimate relationship with an ever-present God. Through his understanding of what Rembrandt had achieved, Blanc was better able to transform a well-established theme, combining everyday elements with basic spirituality. Such melding of humanitarianism and religion made Blanc's work even more appropriate to an age that was witnessing misery on a growing scale.

Although a burgeoning interest in material goods marked Paris in the 1890s and cul-

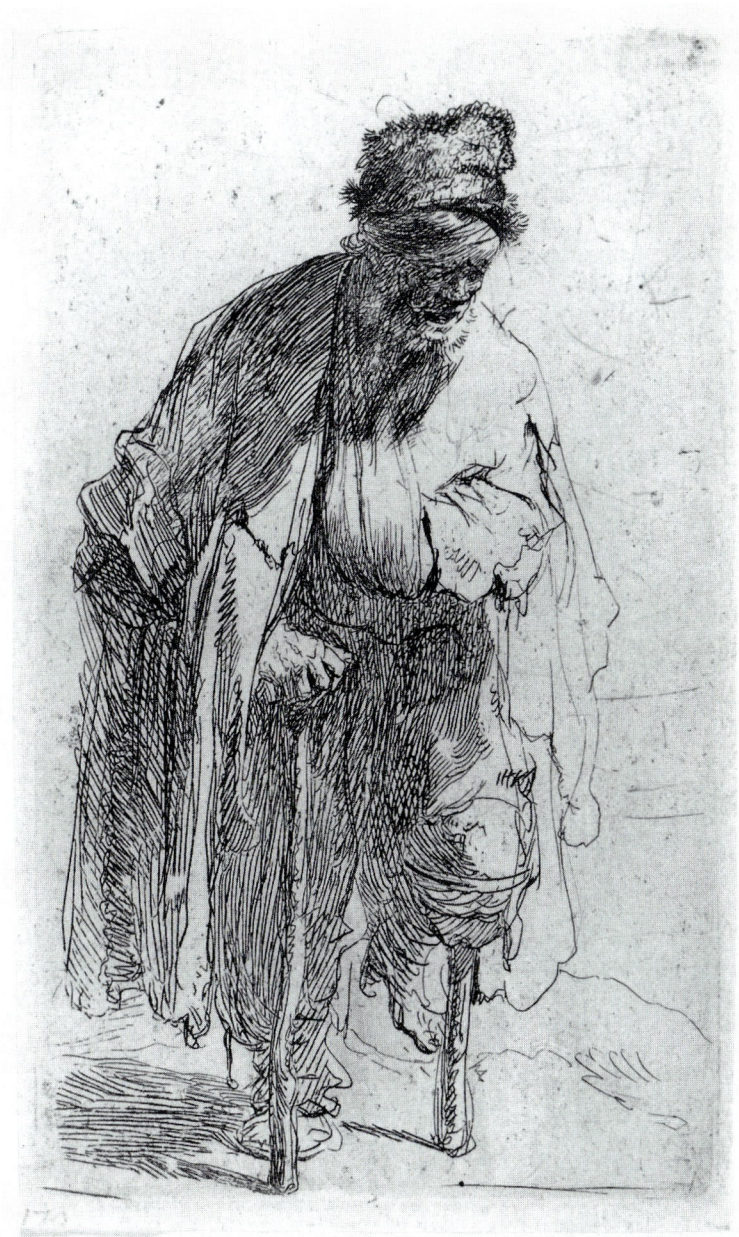

2.4 REMBRANDT VAN RIJN. *Beggar with a Wooden Leg*, 1630 (?). Etching, 11.7 x 7 cm. Minneapolis Institute of Arts, Ladd Collection, gift of Herschel V. Jones, 1916 (P.1301).

minated in the successes associated with the Exposition Universelle of 1900, another side to life existed. Numerous people had been displaced by industrialization. The promise of the innovations and inventions promoted

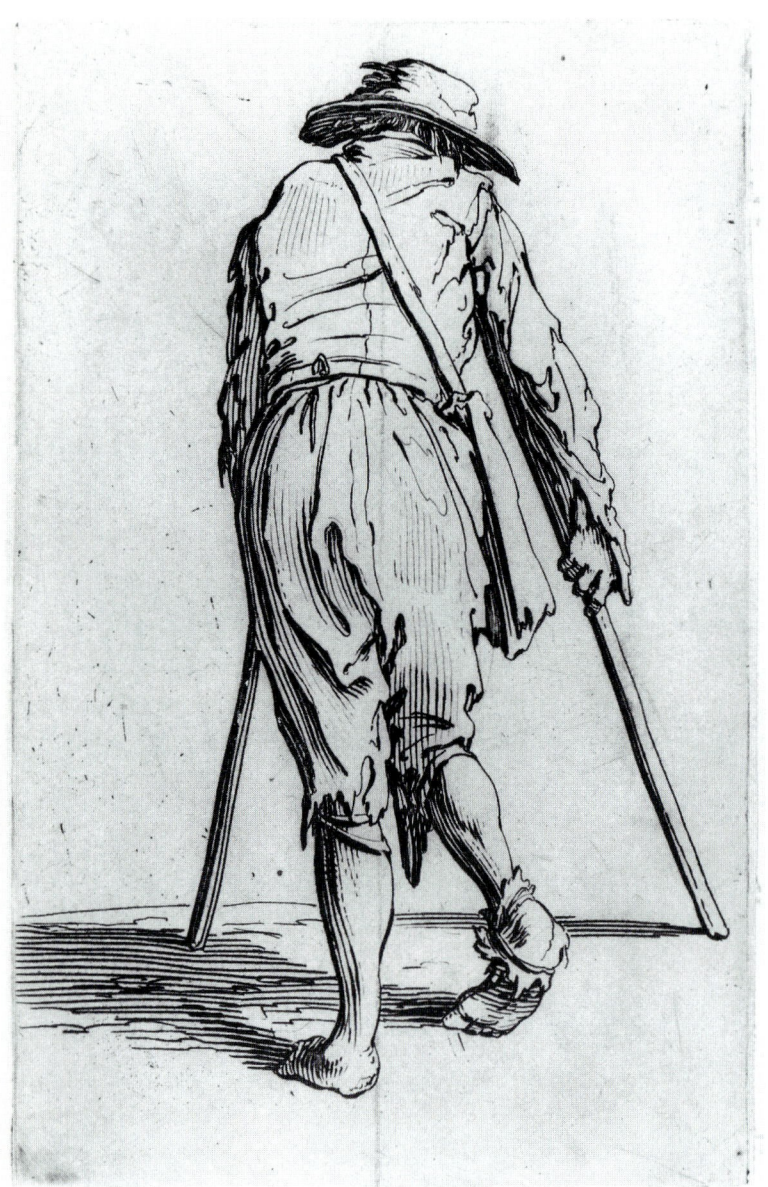

2.5 JACQUES CALLOT. *Beggar on Crutches, Wearing a Hat,* plate 5 of *Les Gueux,* 1622. Etching, 14 x 8.9 cm. Minneapolis Institute of Arts, Lilian Z. Turnblad Fund, 1964 (P.13.221).

Gabriel P. Weisberg

lihood in the visual arts. He participated in the Exposition des artistes marseillais in 1889 and received critical approval, but few works were purchased and no dealer was willing to provide him with needed financial backing. By 1894, Blanc was back in Paris to learn more about early printmakers, to renew his contacts among his artist friends, and especially to arrange a large retrospective of his work. This exhibition of 113 prints established Blanc's imagery within the art circles of Paris.

THE EXPOSITION PAUL BLANC

No records document how many visitors attended Blanc's exhibition; the mere fact that it was held is a tribute to the artist's tenacity and his friendship with Charles Chincholle, a writer for *Le Figaro* who intentionally met Blanc on a trip to the south of France. Chincholle interested others at *Le Figaro* in Blanc's work, particularly the writer Georges Regnal, who persuaded the editor Fernand Clerget to hold the exhibition in his bookstore. This same Georges Regnal, who wrote for *Le Figaro* under the pseudonym of Comtesse Laetitia, wrote the introduction to the exhibition's catalogue. The exhibition attracted the attention of the well-known printmaker Félix Buhot, who asked Chincholle how he could obtain works by Blanc.[21] To advertise Blanc's prints, Chincholle answered Buhot's letter in the pages of *l'Estampe.* Reviews appeared in several magazines, including one in *La Revue des Beaux-Arts et des Lettres* on 15 July 1898. The reviewer, Léon de Saint-Valéry, clearly approved of Blanc's work: "De Rambrandt [*sic*] parfois de Callot, et de Daumier souvent, mais aussi de Hokousai et de son double Hokkei, on se souvient en présence de l'oeuvre gravée de M. Paul Blanc . . . on y perçoit plutôt une personalité farouchement indépendante."[22] After drawing parallels with the

in 1889 and earlier at World's Fairs, those grand symbols of progress, did not translate into better working conditions or plentiful jobs. Blanc conveyed this disappointed atmosphere in his prints, and they spoke to audiences in the provinces and in the capital.

Following his return to France from Italy in the late 1880s, Blanc tried to earn his live-

obvious sources of prints that Blanc had seen (figure 2.5), Saint-Valéry compared him with popular Japanese printmakers—certainly high praise when Japanese prints were all the rage in the mid-1890s. The reviewer then proceeded to discuss some of the fundamental aspects of Blanc's interest in beggars:

M. Blanc ne conçoit pas, le Misérable, la formidable entité sociale, enigmatique, douloureuse, menaçante; il voit des pauvres, une race à part, propagée immuable et pittoresque depuis les lointains des temps, invariable comme un aspect de nature, comme lui impassible, dégageant un peu de tristesse, mais une tristesse imprécise, sensoriale, la tristesse tombée d'un crépuscule très obscur, ou évaporée d'un accord mineur.

Avec son dessin précis, sa science réaliste des attitudes machinales, M. Paul Blanc est un bel animalier traitant du genre homme.[23]

Such sympathetic appraisal of Blanc's work, coming at a time when other artists were also portraying the downtrodden, would have elevated Blanc's work and made it worthy of serious examination. The fact that his work was not being neglected by critics was encouraging; certainly it would have attracted attention in the artistic community. Many would have tried to place his prints within a broader context, seeking out all the works he had created throughout his career and looking for reproductions of *Mendiants,* his lost Salon painting of 1882, a work that was among the first in which he centered attention on a beggar, in this case a blind man attended by a child. This painting, which was reproduced as a print, echoes the popular story of Lazarillo de Tormes accompanied by a blind beggar, a tale portrayed by other painters in the 1870s and 1880s. Its iconic grouping reflects a stiff-

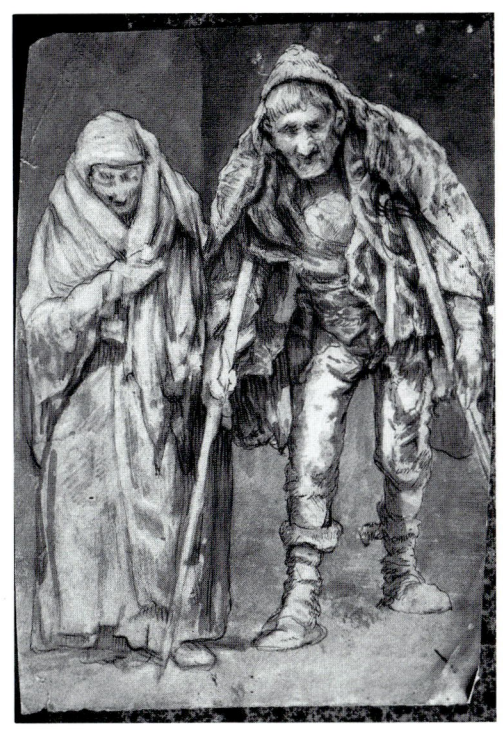

2.6 PAUL BLANC. *Old Beggar on Crutches with Old Beggar Woman.* Pen and white chalk, 25.5 x 17.5 cm. Private collection.

ness of pose that proved of interest to painters in the early twentieth century who likewise became fascinated by such wanderers who moved from town to town in the French countryside.

In keeping with his training at the Ecole des Beaux-Arts, Blanc made preliminary drawings in pen and ink directly from a model. These studies were then developed into etchings. His drawings, which numbered in the hundreds, have not been well preserved over the years. Those that have been located in the possession of the artist's family indicate that Blanc was often obsessed by groupings of beggars. Some figures reappeared throughout his career. Certain drawings focus on the primary figures of *Mendiants.* In others, Blanc modified the older beggar but retained his relationship with the child. It cannot be determined when drawings were completed or whether they were done before or after an oil painting. Nevertheless, Blanc returned to the theme to work

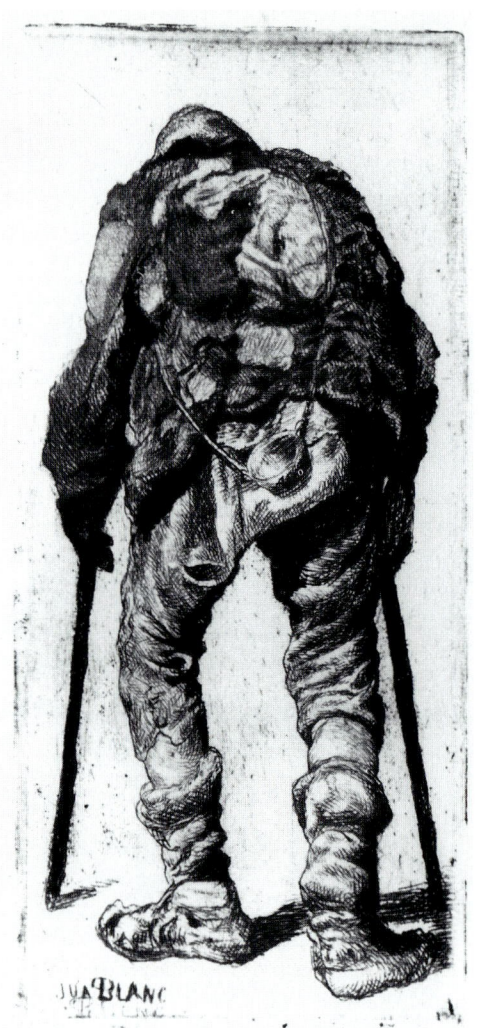

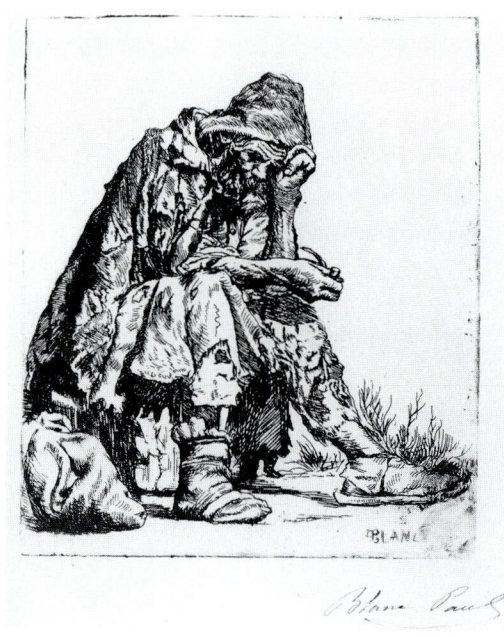

By the mid-1890s, Blanc had created an encyclopedic rendering of all types of beggars, and the best of his etchings were shown at his 1897 exhibition. Among them was the image of a solitary beggar, seen from the back, supporting himself on crutches (figure 2.7). Blanc infused the print with the strong sense of misery and suffering that is being experienced by the handicapped man. The elimination of a background or surrounding environment draws attention to the print's potent message and elicits a sympathetic response. It eventually entered the collection of the Musée des Beaux-Arts in Marseille.[24]

The same beggar reappears in a second etching, *Le Sans Tabac* (figure 2.8), which was included in the 1896 Paris exhibition. Exhausted from his travels, the beggar rests for a few moments, hoping to enjoy his pipe, but his pipe is out and he obviously has no tobacco. Denied this simple pleasure, he becomes a picture of resignation, dejection, and fatigue. In terms of the artist's linear style and his practice of sharply defining figural details, with little play of shadow or sense

out all possible meanings. He also periodically returned to the image of the elderly beggar on crutches and in tattered clothes, occasionally accompanied by a woman (figure 2.6). Some drawings functioned as preliminary studies for etchings; other later drawings, one dated 1901, show that the artist never gave up on a model. He would return to a motif even after the best of his etchings had been completed. His descriptive exactitude toward clothes and posture and the way his models are posed belie his academic training, for he would have learned this craft in the studio of either Meissonier or Gérôme.

of mystery, this work stands out among the others. Its primary purpose is to elucidate the beggar's condition with utmost accuracy.

The close connection between these etchings and their corresponding drawings demonstrates how interrelated all the graphic arts were in Blanc's mind. He likely saw little difference between etchings and pen-and-ink drawings or charcoal studies heightened with gouache. They all allowed him to work on an intimate scale, in keeping with his thoughts. That he did not concern himself with color further suggests that these graphic media well suited his dour theme.

A third etching of a beggar on crutches seen from the front was included in the 1897 exhibition (figures 2.9 and 2.10). Blanc took considerable time to convey the specific likeness of a beggar he most likely knew well personally. Almost certainly the "portrait" shows the same figure who was earlier seen from the rear (figure 2.7). Contributing to the figure's pathetic air are the cap tied around his head, his patched cape made of rags, and his tattered, worn boots. Through this stark portrait study, completed in full illumination, Blanc manages to generate a sense of sympathy for this downcast figure.

The range of Blanc's impact as an artist remains to be determined. Even though a large number of his prints were shown in 1896, and may have attracted a dedicated public audience, were they widely noticed by critics? If so, were people interested in the timeliness of Blanc's theme, or did they consider him an eccentric whose images were decidedly backward in their sentiment and choice of themes? Since Blanc's etchings did appeal to certain printmakers who were working in black-and-white and in a Symbolist mode, such as Félix Buhot, his images and choice of theme were not summarily dismissed. If anything, his close assimilation of subjects depicted by Callot and Rembrandt

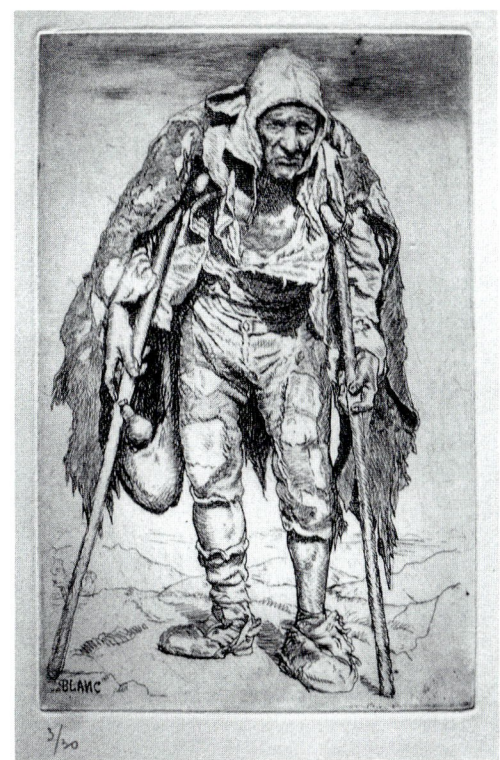

2.9 PAUL BLANC. *Old Beggar on Crutches Seen from the Front,* undated. Pen and gouache, 25.5 x 16.5 cm. Private collection.

2.10 PAUL BLANC. *Old Beggar on Crutches Seen from the Front* (Blanc 31; Blanc/Ripert 2), undated. Etching and drypoint, 21 x 13.5 cm. Private collection.

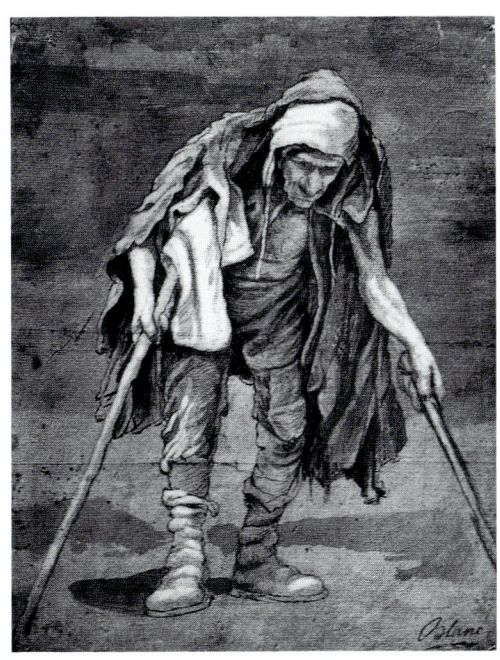

would have been well received, since the work of other printmakers in the 1890s reflected a similar appreciation for these artists. For example, Frank Brangwyn in England and D. Y.

Cameron in Scotland were two printmakers who, in their explorations of beggars, have been compared with Blanc in a most positive way.[25] Even though producing black-and-white etchings was not widely practiced by other printmakers at that time, Blanc would not have appeared behind the times. Indeed, his timely theme of the plight of the homeless would have appeared quite modern, at least to the average print collector and critic of the day.

Interest in the beggar as a theme also attracted other printmakers during the 1890s. Most of those who investigated this side of *belle époque* life, such as Edgar Chahine, worked primarily in lithography.[26] Others who prepared images for the numerous periodicals that then flourished used the homeless family as a symbol for the uncertainty of rural life. They came to represent the problems that affected so many during this period of financial depression and changing work conditions. Yet of those artists who occasionally incorporated images of wanderers into their work, none was so totally absorbed in the theme as Paul Blanc. Depicting beggars in his art became his sole reason for existence.

The availability of Blanc's prints, the timing of an exhibition at a moment of intense interest in the topic of beggars, and his role as a leading proponent of including images of vagabonds in the visual arts all strongly suggest that his work may have been seen and assimilated by younger artists who would come into prominence in the twentieth century. Admittedly, ties with the early works of Pablo Picasso cannot be established with certainty; Picasso could have assimilated the theme of the beggar from a variety of sources. Nevertheless, the fact that Picasso was so taken with different types of beggars at the turn of the century, and particularly during his Blue Period, leads to speculation that he

might have seen, collected, or discussed Blanc's work.[27] Quite likely Blanc was held up as an example of what an artist could accomplish when a personal vision of reality was followed. (After all, he had actually lived as a vagrant himself.) Picasso's sympathy toward those who, like himself, were on the fringe of society could have led to further awareness of Blanc's contribution.[28] If true, it would provide another dimension of influence to an artist whose work seems so appropriate for the late twentieth century.

The impression remains that Blanc was not a romanticist who constructed images of beggars without an actual conception of reality. He was direct in his representation; his candor was based on acute observation and upon a personal familiarity with beggars. His images of vagrants were always filled with a sense of actuality, and yet at the same time his beggars symbolized the uncertainties and misery of life.

This article is dedicated to the memory of Paul Samuels, who, more than ten years ago, introduced me to the work of Paul Blanc. Mr. Samuels was a passionate collector of Blanc's prints, and his enthusiasm for the artist's work has been passed onto others.

NOTES

1. Examination of the career and work of Blanc has been limited to a few studies. For further reference see *Catalogue des 244 sujets composant l'oeuvre gravé de Paul Blanc,* établi par les soins de son fils Valère et de Pierre Ripert (undated); and Jean Marzet, *Paul Blanc et ses mendicanti,* d'après des documents recueillis par Eugène Hoffmann et les fils de l'artiste (Marseille: Chez Valère Blanc, 1959). Among the few worthwhile articles on the artist are Vernon Blake, "Paul Blanc: The Story of a Master Etcher," *Connoisseur Magazine* 60–70 (July 1924): 127–33; and Pierre Ripert, "Paul

Gabriel P. Weisberg

Blanc, peintre et graveur provençal (1836–1910)," *Bulletin Officiel du Musée du Vieux-Marseille*, nos. 30–31 (January-February 1935): 1–16.

In 1896, at the time of Blanc's first major retrospective in Paris, a series of articles was published. These include "Echos," *L'Estampe* (26 August 1896): 1; Ch. Chincholle, "L'Oeuvre du graveur Paul Blanc," *L'Estampe* (14 March 1897): 1; "Exposition Paul Blanc," *L'Estampe et L'Affiche* (15 December 1897): 63; and Nicolas Manoff, "Souvenirs d'Artiste" (September 1897): 176–79 and (15 December 1897): 199–201. A later article was prepared on Blanc's contribution, noting how his work could be summed up in one word: beggars. For reference see Nicolas Manoff, "Blanc Paul et son oeuvre," *L'Estampe* (19 September 1900): 3 and (24 September 1900): 3–4. Interest in beggars, wanderers, and vagabonds reached a fevered pitch by 1900 and encompassed not only the world of art but also political strategies and social assistance programs for the indigent.

2. Marzet, 30–36.

3. Ibid., 36. The closeness of the relationship with Regnault demonstrates a friendship with one of the leading young achievers at the Ecole des Beaux-Arts.

4. Ibid., 53–64.

5. For reference to *Mendiants*, see *Catalogue du Salon des Artistes Français* (Paris 1882), no. 278. This painting has since disappeared, although the artist did reproduce it as an etching. For a reproduction see Marzet, 59.

6. Blanc's relation to both Callot and Rembrandt is cited in Blake, 128. The theme of the beggar as ragpicker is discussed in Catherine Jean Kudlick, "Disease, Public Health, and Urban Social Relations: Perceptions of Cholera and the Paris Environment, 1830–1850" (Ph.D. diss., University of California, Berkeley, 1988), 195–203. The ragpicker became a significant symbol of "Paris malade" and further reinforced the idea that those dangerous elements in society that were being threatened were in response becoming more reactionary. Consideration of the issues surrounding the destitute is reflected in numerous serious studies on the condition of beggars in the late nineteenth and early twentieth centuries. Among these works are MM. Marie et Hamel, *Vagabondage et folie* (Rouen: Impr. Cagniard [Léon Gy, successeur], 1898), in which the authors try to find reasons for the presence of so many beggars. They address the issue of mental health, since numerous beggars were unable to change their lifestyles. Other studies, such as Léon Lefebure, *Les Sans-travail, la lutte contre le vagabondage et la mendicité* (Paris, 1896), examined differences between genuine beggars and those who were not. Lefebure advocated creating a large bureaucratic organization that would regulate indigency and process valid claims for public assistance. By 1911 Paul Blanc (no relation to the printmaker) published his doctoral dissertation on "La Vie mendiante et vagabondage" (University of Grenoble, Avallon, 1911). As a "commissaire de Police," this Blanc knew indigency at firsthand.

7. After meeting with members of Blanc's family and gaining access to works still in their possession, I can document that no other theme mattered to the artist. On this point, see Manoff, "Blanc Paul et son oeuvre," and his comment that "tout l'oeuvre se résume en un mot: *les Mendiants*" (p. 3).

8. See *Des diverses catégories de mendiants* (undated), a manuscript by Paul Blanc, now in the possession of the artist's descendants. The manuscript may have been largely completed by the late 1890s. See also Marzet, 107–8.

9. Marzet, 107–8.

10. For reference to this presentation in December 1896, see the exhibition catalogue *L'Oeuvre du graveur Blanc Paul*, chez l'Editeur F. Clerget, 17 rue Guenegaud, Paris. This two-page flyer functioned as a brief, annotated catalogue of the 112 images of beggars. It is not known how widely the flyer was distributed; reviews of the exhibition were not extensive.

On the question of the infestation of beggars throughout cities and the countryside, see, for example, Ferdinand Moine, *Une plaie sociale, la mendicité, le mal, le remède* (Paris/Bordeaux, 1901). Moine wrote that "nos villes et nos campagnes, en effet, sont infestées de nomades sans aveu, de loqueteux opiniâtres, de va-nu-pieds sans patrie, de vagabonds déguenillés, pour qui les arrêtés de préfets sont lettres mortes pour qui les lois n'existent pas." Moine was also obsessed with dividing beggars into types so they could be treated by society. He noted that some beggars contributed to moral decay because they were totally undermined by alcoholism or had no basic character.

11. Among the many books in existence was *Le Vagabond ou l'Histoire et le caractère de la malice et des fourberies de ceux qui courent le monde aux dépens d'autruy*. First published in Italy in 1627, this book was translated into French and published in Paris in 1644. While this is not the earliest text in France, England, or Germany to chronicle the life of beggars, it does serve as a good example of the type of texts that were available on the theme. It portrayed beggars as wanderers who roamed the countryside without roots to one locale. It also cautioned that beggars could be dangerous. A large part of the text examined a wide range of specific types: those who were liars, those who falsely represented themselves as monks, and those who saw themselves as sinners and were revealing God's justice until they were saved. The presence of beggars in society served as a reminder of sin and the consequences of transgression.

Other early texts that address this theme include *Liber Vagatorum*, published between 1509 and 1520. For reference to this book, see *The Book of Vagabonds and Beggars with a Vocabulary of Their Language and a Preface by Martin Lüther* (London, 1932). For additional information and insight, see contained in C. J. Ribton-Turner, *A History of Vagrants and Vagrancy and Beggars and Begging* (reprint, Montclair, N.J.: 1972).

12. One of the best known of these novels was *The Life of Lazarillo de Tormes, His Fortunes and Adversities*, first published in 1554. This novel was of considerable interest to nineteenth-century realist artists. For reference to this changing attitude, see Alexandre Vexliard, *Introduction à la sociologie du vagabondage* (Paris, 1956), especially the section "le vagabond face à la répression," 82–92.

13. For reference to these effects see Ferdinand-Dreyfus, *Misères sociales et études historiques* (Paris, 1901), 97–111.

14. For a representation of the beggar as a rogue, see Lucinda Kate Reinold, "The Representation of the Beggar as Rogue in Dutch Seventeenth-Century Art" (Ph.D. diss., University of California, Berkeley, 1981). For a discussion of the sense of compassion toward the beggar, see Robert W. Baldwin, "'On earth we are beggars, as Christ himself was': The Protestant Background of Rembrandt's Imagery of Poverty, Disability, and Begging," *Konsthistorik tidskrift* 54 (1985): 122–35.

15. Baldwin, 122.

16. The general attitude of intolerance is discussed in Suzanne Stratton, "Rembrandt's Beggars: Satire and Sympathy," *Print Collector's Newsletter* 27, no. 3 (July-August 1986): 78–82. A contemporary examination of beggars is found in Nicholas Dawidoff, "The Business of Begging," *New York Times Magazine*, 24 April 1994, 34–41, 50–52.

17. Baldwin, 123.

18. Lüther, *Works*, as noted by Baldwin, "'On earth we are beggars,'" 127. Further examination of the biblical aspects of poverty is found in Leo Brummel, "Lüther and the Biblical Language of Poverty," *Ecumenical Review* (1980): 40–48.

19. Corrie, G. E., ed., *The Works of Hugh Latimer*, (Cambridge, 1844): 2:126–27.

20. Blanc became a great student of Rembrandt's prints, some of which he examined at the print collection of the Bibliothèque nationale. For reference to the book used by Blanc, see *Notes tirées du Catalogue raisonné de toutes les estampes . . .* (Paris, 1824).

21. For reference to this exhibition and the involvement of F. Clerget, see Marzet, 122–23. The short, untitled preface by Georges Regnal took up one column of the small catalogue/pamphlet that was prepared for the Blanc exhibition. Clerget, unfortunately, sold only twenty-two prints from the exhibition. On this see Marzet, 144–47. On Buhot's interest see Marzet, 144–47.

22. Léon de Saint-Valéry, "Exposition de M. Paul Blanc, Galerie F. Clerget, 13 boulevard Montparnasse," *La Revue des Beaux-Arts et des Lettres* (15 July 1898): 374. As noted in this review, Blanc was compared with other artist-printmakers in earlier periods as well as with artists of the nineteenth century. The other major artistic influence on Blanc was Jacques Callot. As he had done for Rembrandt, Blanc recorded his personal impressions of the life and work of Callot, writing, "Il avait la passion de créer des gueux, . . . comme d'autres ont celle de jouer, c'était presque de l'ivresse. . . . Venu après Albert Dürer et avant Rembrandt, Callot malgré tout son génie, s'efface un peu entre ces deux grands maîtres dans l'art de graver et de peindre." Since it is possible to document Callot's importance for Rembrandt, we have a perfect lineage from Callot to Rembrandt to Blanc. For Callot see *Jacques Callot (1592–1635)* (exh. cat., Paris, 1992).

23. Saint-Valéry, 374.

24. Blanc's relationship with the Musée Longchamp in Marseille began in 1907 when the city purchased ten etchings from the artist. These had ostensibly been shown in 1906 at the Exposition coloniale in Marseille. For reference to these prints see Longchamp, Inv. nos. G 127–36. The prices paid for the prints ranged from fifteen to forty francs. Further reference to Blanc's ties with the museum are found in Pierre Ripert, "Paul Blanc, peintre et graveur provençal, 1836–1910," *Bulletin Officiel du Musée du Vieux-Marseille,* nos. 30–31 (January-February 1935): 1–16.

25. The relationship between Blanc and Frank Brangwyn is noted in Léon Mouche, "Paul Blanc— Graveur provençal (1836–1910)," typescript, conveyed to the author by Blanc's descendants in Marseille. It is possible that this article was never published, but Mouche published at least one article on Blanc in *Le Radical de Marseille* on 19 October 1928.

26. For reference to Edgar Chahine's strong interest in beggar themes see M. R. Tabanelli, *Edgar Chahine, Catalogue de l'oeuvre gravé* (Milan: Il Mercante de Stampe, Editeur, 1974). See also Gabriel P. Weisberg, *Edgar Chahine, Le vie parisienne* (Washington, D.C.: Smithsonian Institution Traveling Exhibition Service, 1984).

27. For Picasso's depiction of poverty and misery as it affected small family groups and for the examination of themes and symbols of misfortune, see Patricia Leighton, *Re-Ordering the Universe, Picasso and Anarchism, 1897–1914* (Princeton: Princeton University Press, 1989): 24–47. Picasso's familiarity with all types of popular and public graphic imagery is well known. Since he was also obsessed with the theme of abject poverty and the social problems that developed from indigency, it is possible that he could have sought out other works by artists who had utilized the theme.

28. Leighton, 24–47.

3 | FORUMS OF THE ABSURD

Three Avant-Garde Lithographic Publications

at the Turn of the Last Century

PHILLIP DENNIS CATE

THERE WAS AN ASPECT OF RADICAL, anti-academic activity among artists and writers in France at the end of the nineteenth century that was essentially collaborative in nature and that prefigured twentieth-century concerns of Dadaism, Surrealism, and Fluxus in particular, and conceptual art in general. This activity, first manifested at the end of the 1870s and in the 1880s by the groups called the Hydropathes and the Incohérents dissolved barriers that demarcated the visual arts, literature, performance, and music. A Rabelaisian humor based on parody and the absurd was its primary common denominator. The academic painter Jean Léon Gérome is said to have called the Incohérents "the anarchists of art."[1] This "anarchic," multimedia art paralleled other avant-garde activities dominated by Impressionist and Post-Impressionist painting. It also included among its participants some members of these better-known groups such as Edouard Vuillard and Pierre Bonnard of the Nabis. However, because much of its activity resulted in literary-artistic ephemera and performance and was, by some of its artists' own admission, "not serious," its relevance to art history has been under appreciated. The participation within this unusual aesthetic phenomenon of traditional art media, including printmaking, was relatively small. In fact, printed images by the artists involved were normally combined with texts and printed photomechanically in paperbacks or journals on pulp stock.

The two rather obscure publications discussed below and Alfred Jarry's 1901 *Almanach du Père Ubu* are prime examples of fin-de-siècle art of the absurd. They are extraordinary within this genre of the avant-garde precisely because they use lithography as the vehicle for their challenge to traditional artistic values.

Le Fond de Bain (The Dregs of the Bath) (1895–98) and *L'Omnibus de Corinthe (The Omnibus of Corinth)* (1896–98) were created as "journals" by the artists Hermann René Georges Paul, called Hermann-Paul (1864–1940), and Marc Mouclier (1866–1948), respectively. The formats for presenting humor—short-dialogue jokes, puns, sexual innuendos, rebuses, and the incorporation of pseudonyms—in these two publications have obvious precedents in the *Chat noir* of the 1880s and in *La Vie drole, Le Chasseur de Chevelures, Nib*, and other journals of the 1890s.[2] Although conventional procedures for journals, such as editors, publishers, subscription rates, and so on, theoretically existed for *Le Fond de Bain* and *L'Omnibus de Corinthe*, they are not journals in the real sense of the word; rather, they are serial manifestations of a collaborative literary-artistic art based on humor. The artists appropriated the journal format for the expression of the absurd and of their own graphic art, yet they rejected the industrial, photomechanical printing technique normally associated with contempo-

rary illustrated journals in favor of the traditional artistic medium of lithography, creating, in the end, very personal statements. Alfred Jarry, on the other hand, chose the almanac as the forum for his fourth cycle, or presentation, of Père Ubu, a character synonymous with human absurdities. The *Almanach du Père Ubu* contains similar shock-value obscenities and embodies the outrageous stupidities introduced in the theatrical production of *Ubu Roi*, first performed in December 1896 at the Théâtre de l'Oeuvre. Just as Jarry created the theater of the absurd with costumes and stage set designs by Paul Sérusier, Henri de Toulouse-Lautrec, Vuillard, Paul Ranson, and Bonnard, and with music by Claude Terrasse, he also invented an almanac of the absurd with lithographs by Bonnard and a score by Terrasse.[3]

Each of the three publications under discussion clearly states its commitment to humor and to the absurd. In the second issue of *Le Fond de Bain*, for example, a character named Van Der Bilt exclaims, "Your journal is idiotic. No one understands it!" Three years later in its last issue, the editors' farewell address notes that in opposition to journalists who deal with sensational and titillating news, "they [the editors] preferred to write down with no rhyme or reason all their passing fantasies"; but that "some readers found their method a little infantile." In the inaugural issue of *L'Omnibus de Corinthe*, Emile Straus, writing under the alias of Martine, observes "that a man of spirit wishing to perpetuate 'la vieille gaité francaise' found in the now defunct *Chasseurs de Chevelures, Nib* and other 'concombreries' [cucumberies], resolutely kicks himself in the 'calebasse' [head] to devise a paper which brings joy as its profit. This man is Marc Mouclier. He hopes to associate with his paper the syndicate of 'Esprit gaulois' in all its

Phillip
Dennis Cate

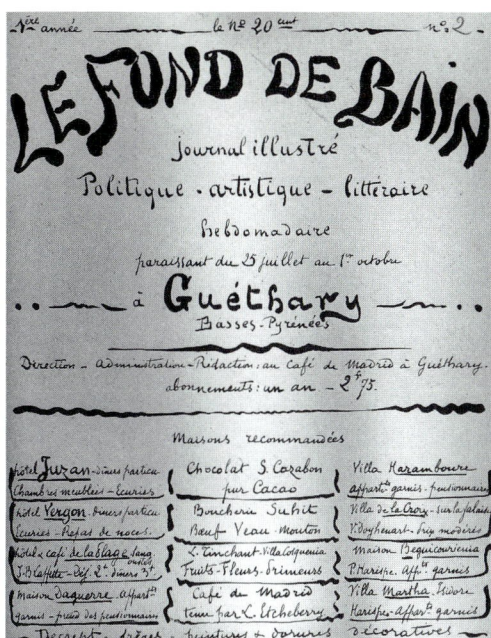

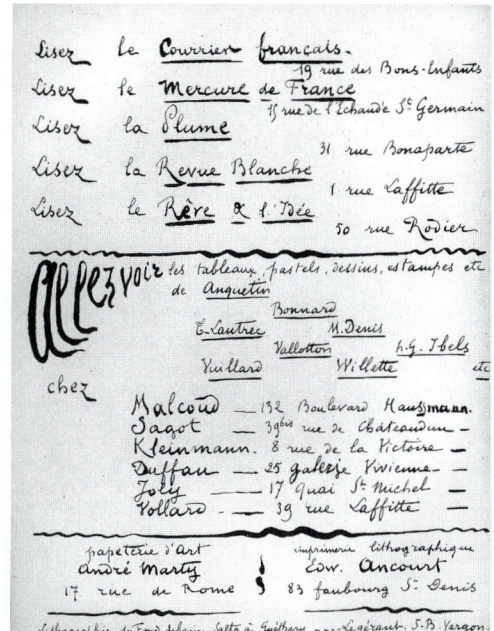

splendor, the patented entrepreneurs of laughter." Finally, in an announcement in *La Revue blanche* of 1 January 1901, Jarry predicts that the *Almanach du Père Ubu* will reveal that "Ubu's absurdity follows a logic more irrefutable than that of a fool or a senile person."[4]

Le Fond de Bain (figures 3.1, 3.2) and *L'Omnibus de Corinthe* (figure 3.3) share a number of elements in common. In both, lithography is not only the medium for the journals' illustrations, but it is also employed in place of the usual letterpress type for the text. Second, while both are published over a period of several years, the actual total number of issues is relatively small: twenty-one for *Le Fond de Bain*, nine for *L'Omnibus de Corinthe*. Third, a deluxe limited edition of each journal was printed on Japan or Holland paper. Hermann-Paul, in fact, had twelve proofs of each of his ten images from 1895 printed on deluxe paper and sold as a set of ten prints for ten francs. These elements, together, take the publications out of the usual

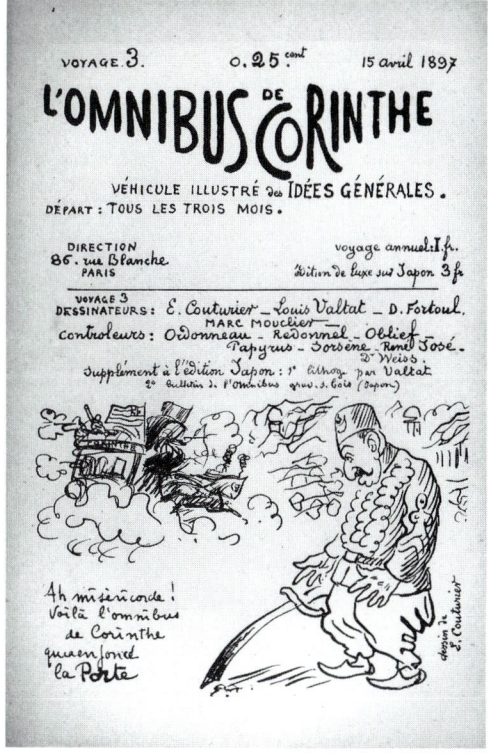

domain of the journal and into the domain of innovative works of art on paper. Fourth, unlike Bonnard's illustrations for Jarry's almanac, the lithographic images of the two journals rarely relate directly to their text. Fifth, pseudonyms or aliases are used in both journals by the artists and writers as a means to impart their sought-after absurd character. Sixth, each journal, by means of its back-page ads, visibly (and, thus, philosophically) aligns itself and its infantile humor with prominent, contemporary, literary-artistic journals such as *La Revue blanche, La Critique, Le Mercure de France,* and *La Plume.* This association with sophisticated and successful journals bears witness to the fact that *Le Fond de Bain* and *L'Omnibus de Corinthe* had a high degree of artistic credibility within Parisian avant-garde circles.

The first ten issues of *Le Fond de Bain* were published weekly from 25 July 1895 to 1 October 1895 by Hermann-Paul during his summer retreat from Paris at Guéthary on the southwest coast of France. That the publication was intended both for specialized, Parisian audiences and for the local and tourist populations of the resort town is indicated by the numerous references to Parisian notables, places, and events within the journal's text and by the advertisements on the back cover. It was at some of the establishments promoted in these ads that *Le Fond de Bain* could be purchased in Paris. One assumes that the journal also received some financial support from the hotels and restaurants in the Basses-Pyrénées in exchange for listings on the front covers in 1895 and 1896. The "gérant," or manager, of the paper was J. B. Vergon of the Vergon Hotel, while the office of the "directors" of the journal was the Café de Madrid, owned by a Madame Etcheberry. The lithographic printer of *Le Fond de Bain* was listed first as "Salto à Guéthary" and later as "J. Clureau, Bayonne." During the three years in which the journal was published, an increasing number of nonsensical articles and references were related to the events and people of the region.

Paul created a total of thirty-two lithographs for the journal, one for each of the ten issues of 1895, two for the single 1896 issue, and two for each of the ten issues of its final year, 1898 (the journal was not published in 1897). While the images for the first two years deal with social satire, the twenty images for 1898 are equally divided between social and political commentary, with the former appearing on the front cover and the latter on the back. Typically the subject of Paul's social, satirical art is the bourgeoisie; in his lithographs for *Le Fond de Bain,* he depicts the human comedy of middle-class tourists summering in Guéthary, from their arrival to their departure and all the joys in between. His political images for the journal give a regional emphasis to Spain and to subjects of Spanish and American colonialism. Essentially, Paul's lithographs for *Le Fond de Bain* do not depart stylistically or thematically from his other work.[5] What makes this journal so unusual, therefore, is that each of the first eleven issues was drawn lithographically by Paul. It is an orthographic work of art as intimate and spontaneous as a personal letter in that mistakes and corrections are retained. *L'Omnibus de Corinthe* shares this handwritten quality, except that more than one artist was involved. This seemingly amateurish approach may be found in humorous, student publications of the period, and on a smaller scale, it had been used by artists such as T. A. Steinlen and Adolphe Willette in illustrations for journals of the 1880s, such as *Le Chat noir* and *Le Courrier français.* However, Paul's calligraphic and rhythmic style of writing takes on a graphic sophistication that is compatible with the artistic experimentation of his Parisian peers with whom he was actively involved and to whom he makes direct reference in the ads on the back cover: Louis Anquetin, Bonnard, Toulouse-Lautrec, Maurice Denis, Félix Vallotton, Henri Ibels, Vuillard, and Willette. In fact, Paul's ad recalls the linear, orthographic style of Bonnard's 1894 poster for *La Revue Blanche*.

Paul used the pseudonym "Agapito" when he signed his lithographic images for the ten 1895 images of *Le Fond de Bain*. He is also referred to by this alias within the text. He signed the two images for the 1896 issue with the monogram of his real name, Hermann-Paul, although within the text he is still referred to as Agapito. It was not until the first issue of 1898 that he is fully identified as Hermann-Paul. Because of the constant use of aliases in combination with absurd humor in the text, it is difficult to determine if Paul is solely responsible for the journal's content or if, in fact, as the text implies, there was a team of editors. For instance, a notice in the 1896 issue states facetiously that "the two principal collaborators of the journal, M. M. Deibler and Paul Hipp," were so enthusiastic about the visit that summer of the Russian Tzar to France that they were unable to return to Guéthary; therefore, the timid Agapito would not dare to produce the journal on his own. Yet, it was apparently Paul who produced that year's sole issue. At one point, the journal states that "Hermann-Paul" has nothing to do with the "direction du *Le Fond de Bain*," and then five issues later, instructs its readers to send subscription payments to the "Direction" by addressing such correspondence "à M. Hermann-Paul à Guéthary, ou à M. Charles Colin, à Ciboure." It seems likely that *Le Fond de Bain* was, at least for the first eleven issues, the creation of one, primary, literary-artistic mind—Hermann-Paul—possibly with editorial assistance from anonymous contributors.

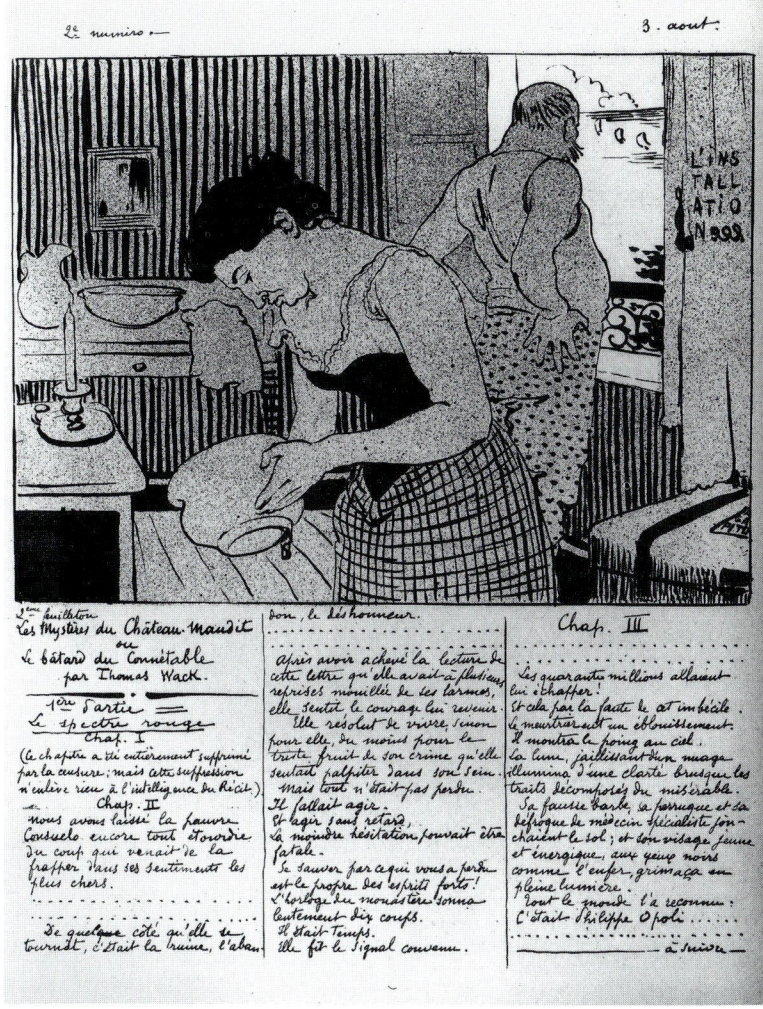

Paul's ten black-and-white images for 1895 are consistently bold compositions with contours richly printed in black, with dense applications of *crachis* (figure 3.4). The journal's texts for 1895 and 1896 were written by one hand, supposedly Paul's, and the ironic humor during these two years is at its sharpest and most original. In 1898, distinct changes occurred that lowered the quality of *Le Fond de Bain*'s aesthetic and intellectual presentation. The style of Paul's lithographs changed to loosely drawn images that, in general, lack the visual impact of the earlier work. In addition, the text for the 1898 issues was printed

3.4 RENE GEORGES HERMANN-PAUL. *Le Fond de Bain* No. 2, 3 August 1895. Lithograph. Zimmerli Art Museum, Herbert Littman purchase fund (84.047.107).

Forums of the Absurd

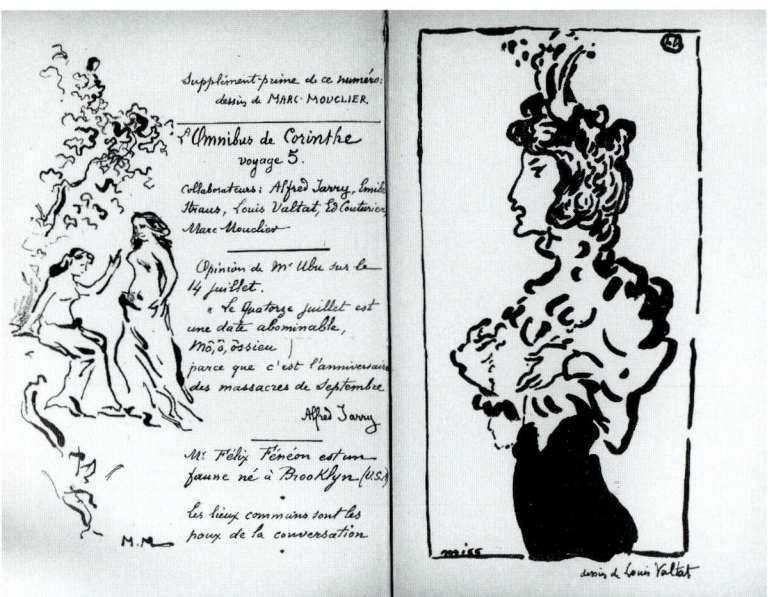

There is no ambiguity about those responsible for *L'Omnibus de Corinthe.* The artist Marc Mouclier was the initiator and "Directeur-gérant" of the eight-page journal. Mouclier, a prolific printmaker, was also a close friend of Bonnard and Vuillard, with whose prints his black-and-white lithographs have much in common stylistically. He also collaborated with George Bans on the latter's literary-artistic journal *La Critique,* which was founded in 1895.[7] In fact, Mouclier relied strongly on his colleagues, such as the artists Louis Valtat, E. Couturier, and Désiré Fortoul from *La Critique,* for each issue of *L'Omnibus de Corinthe* (figure 3.5). Emile Straus, the chief editor of *La Critique,* became the principal voice of *L'Omnibus de Corinthe* under the dual pseudonyms "Papyrus" and "Martine." George Bans and writers Madeline Lépine, Alcanter de Brahm (alias "Oblief"), Willy (Henri Gautier-Villars), André Ibels, Paul Redonnel, and Charles Fuinel also contributed to Mouclier's unusual publication. The nine issues have no consistent format for arrangement of image and text; even the front cover was redrawn each time and, therefore, varies slightly. Closest compositional and stylistic equivalents are Bonnard's and Vuillard's lithographic designs for Théâtre de l'Oeuvre programs.[8]

by letterpress, which deprives it of the earlier personal, spontaneous quality. Finally, the content itself is pat, more pedantic; gone is the ridiculous and ironic humor found in the 1895 issues represented by the serial novelette "Le Batard du Connétable" by "Thomas Wack."[6] Entire passages of this story are literally left blank; chapters are omitted, and sentences are incomplete because, as the author explains, the "sordid" contents were suppressed by the censors. However, according to the author, "this suppression takes nothing away from the intelligibility of the story." The absurdity of this situation is reinforced and amplified by the lavish amount of space allotted to the story within the four-page journal and by Paul's hand-written text in which the gaps due to "censorship" are vividly rendered. "Le Batard du Connétable" is, in fact, a tour de force of early conceptual art. Indeed, there is really no other explanation for the creation of *Le Fond de Bain* than as a form of artistic expression. But by 1898, *Le Fond de Bain* lost its initial artistic resolve and became similar to other, less adventurous, humorous journals.

While Paul's title, *The Dregs of the Bath,* is a relatively simple play on words that refers to both the irregular humor of his journal and the seashore of Guéthary, the allusions in the title *The Omnibus of Corinth* are more complicated. The metaphorical meaning of "Omnibus" is, however, made clear in the subtitle on the journal's front cover: "véhicule illustré des idées générales." The allusion to the transport of ideas is repeated on the eight remaining front covers with the use of the term "voyage" rather than the abbreviation "no." to refer to the issue numbers of the journal and with the use of the word "controleurs" (ticket takers) to refer to the literary "contributors" to each issue.

In 1878 Emile Goudeau, the founder of the Hydropathes, the Hirsutes, and of the journal *Chat noir*, wrote the poem *Les Grecs*.[9] Within the poem's narrative, time and place move between ancient Athens and contemporary Paris; the poem suggests similarities between the two "decadent" societies. The title, *L'Omnibus de Corinthe*, also draws a parallel between the society of ancient Greece and that of contemporary France. As Papyrus explains to Martine in the first issue of the journal, to create *L'Omnibus de Corinthe*, one "graphe un topo sur une gazette révélatrice, rénovatrice, astringente et restringente [*sic*] des antiques humories [*sic*]" (draws an article on a revealing, renovating, astringent and restringent gazette of ancient jokes).

The city of Corinth represents the source of the "antiques humories" of this "gazette" and is the ancient counterpart to fin-de-siècle Paris. Therefore, the Parisian equivalent to the "antiques humories" is that basic Rabelaisian humor, that is, "la vieille gaité française" and "L'Esprit gaulois," which Mouclier wished to perpetuate in his journal. Unfortunately, it was probably due to this rather vague raison d'etre and to its infrequent publication that *L'Omnibus de Corinthe* folded on 15 October 1898 after its ninth voyage.

On the evening of 9 December 1896 at the Théatre de l'Oeuvre in Montmartre, Alfred Jarry's *Ubu Roi* was performed for the first time on stage by actors and not by puppets. The nonsensical production scandalized the audience with its language, its irrational childlike humor, the erratic physical actions of its protagonists, and its overall amoral-apolitical premise. It broke completely with traditional stage and costume design and theatrical decorum. It was an exaggeration to the extreme

of the antithetical schools of French naturalism and symbolism that had dominated avant-garde theater since the establishment of the Théatre Libre in 1887 and Théatre de l'Art in 1890. Its anarchic character challenged not only French academic and, heretofore, French avant-garde literature and theater but also society as a whole.

Jarry was briefly associated with *L'Omnibus de Corinthe*. In voyage five of 15 October 1897, not only was Jarry one of the "collaborators" of the journal, but Couturier drew one of the earliest depictions of Père Ubu not designed by Jarry himself. The next issue, 15 January 1898, included caricatures of Père Ubu by Couturier and by André Ibels, in which the latter made satirical reference to the French colonization of Madagascar. Imperialism in the form of colonization was a target of much fin-de-siècle parody and is found in both *Le Fond de Bain* and *L'Omnibus de Corinthe*. It is also a fundamental theme of *Ubu Roi* and, therefore, plays an important role in *L'Almanach du Père Ubu*.

In *Le Flaneur des deux rives*, Guillaume Apollinaire (1880–1918) notes: "It is in the basement of the rue Laffitte that the *Grand Almanach illustré* was composed. Everyone knows that the authors of it are Alfred Jarry for the text, Bonnard for the illustrations and Claude Terrasse for the music. As for the song, it is by M. Ambroise Vollard. Everyone knows that but no one seems to have remarked that the *Grand Almanach illustré* had been published without the names of the authors or its publisher."[10] *L'Almanach du Père Ubu* is also referred to as the *Grand Almanach illustré* to distinguish it from Jarry's smaller almanac of 1899. Both publications were written by Jarry, illustrated by Bonnard, and published by Vollard, but as Apollinaire notes, the 1901 large *almanach* gives no indication of its creators or publisher nor does the

3.6 Pierre Bonnard. Cover: *Almanach du Père Ubu,* 1901. Lithograph. Zimmerli Art Museum, acquired with the Herbert D. and Ruth Schimmel museum library fund (1994.0169.001).

3.7 Pierre Bonnard. Center spread: *Almanach du Pere Ubu,* 1901. Lithograph. Zimmerli Art Museum, acquired with the Herbert D. and Ruth Schimmel museum library fund (1994.0169.001).

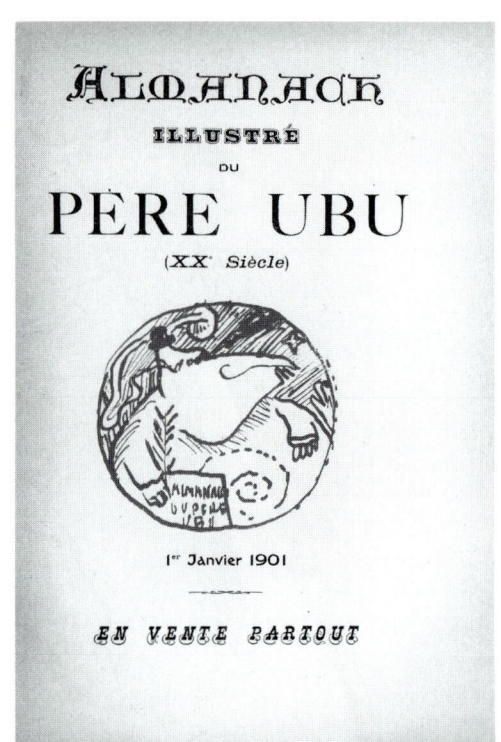

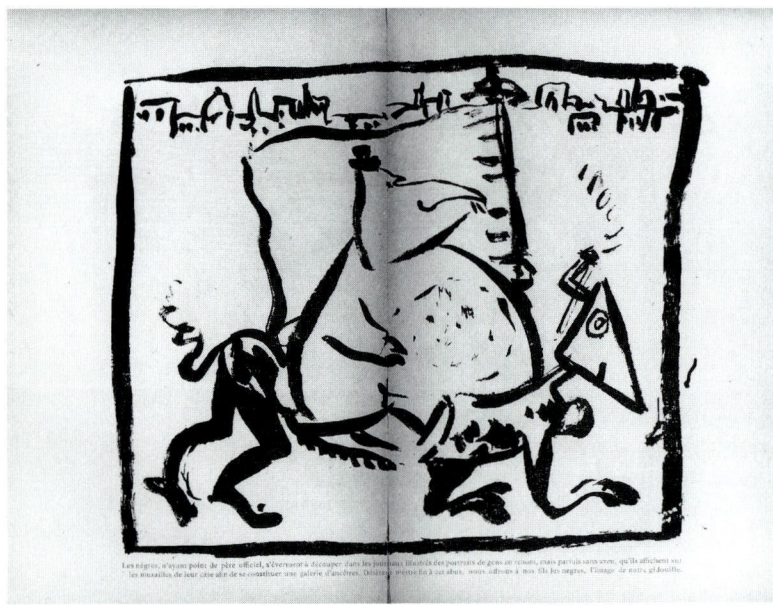

graphically and, in this case, either in red, blue, or black. The text is letterpress and was printed after the paper was run through the lithographic press. While an edition of a thousand on regular stock was projected for the large almanac, it was, in fact, much more limited in number; in addition, twenty-five copies were printed on Japan and on Holland paper each.[11]

Jarry and Bonnard knew of each other as early as 1894 when the former critiqued the latter's painting in his review of the sixth exhibition at the gallery Barc de Boutteville.[12] In 1898 *Le Mercure de France* published a set of nine lithographic sheet music covers for Jarry's *Répertoire des pantins,* six of which were by Bonnard and three by Jarry himself. Bonnard's seventy-nine lithographic images for the large *Almanach du Père Ubu* are the visual counterpart to Jarry's absurd text; flaunting all academic standards, Bonnard gave free reign to his imagination in the interpretation of Jarry's childlike, amoral humor and parody of French society. The spontaneous and crudely drawn images appear throughout the text as scattered vignettes; on one page they intermingle with the text they describe, while elsewhere they are isolated, full-page graphic innovations (figures 3.7, 3.8, 3.9). They are Bonnard's most far-reaching aesthetic excursions into abstraction and visual puns. As some of the most expressive examples of fin-de-siècle art of the absurd, Bonnard's lithographs for *L'Almanach du Père Ubu* opened the twentieth century with an innovative, psychosexual, visual vocabulary that predicted the stylistic and contextual concerns of Pablo Picasso and Henri Matisse, as well as those of the Dadaists and Surrealists.

Le Fond de Bain, L'Omnibus de Corinthe, and *L'Almanach du Père Ubu* demonstrate, in progressively greater degrees, a unification of text and image in the creation of an art of the

earlier smaller almanac (figure 3.6). Unlike Paul's and Mouclier's journals, only the illustrations, and not the text, of Jarry's 1901 *L'Almanach du Père Ubu* are printed litho-

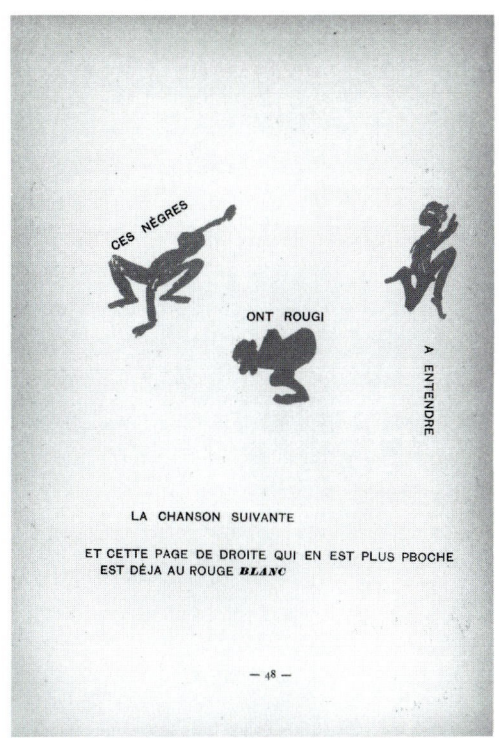

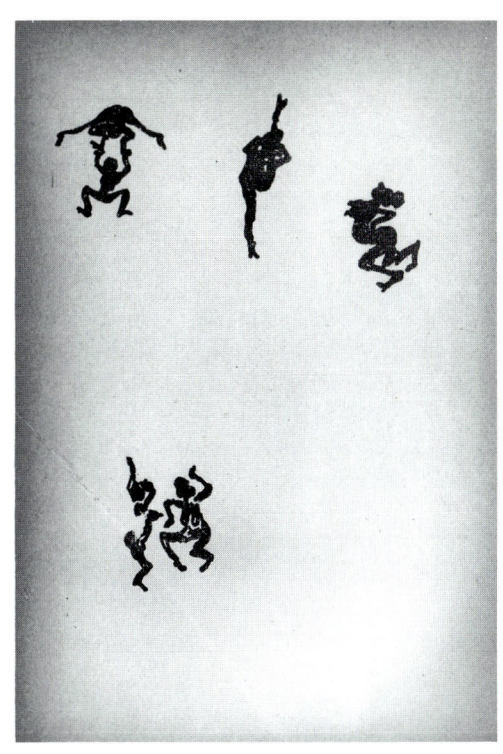

3.8 PIERRE BONNARD.
Illustrations: *Almanach du Pere Ubu*, 1901.
Lithograph. Zimmerli Art Museum, acquired with the Herbert D. and Ruth Schimmel museum library fund (1994.0169.001).

3.9 PIERRE BONNARD.
Illustrations: *Almanach du Pere Ubu*, 1901.
Lithograph. Zimmerli Art Museum, acquired with the Herbert D. and Ruth Schimmel museum library fund (1994.0169.001).

absurd. With Jarry and Bonnard as important contacts between the avant-garde of the end of the nineteenth century and that of the next generation, it seems apparent that much ephemeral, fin-de-siècle art of the absurd was available to and known by early pioneers of twentieth-century radical art. For example, Picasso, at one point, owned Hermann-Paul's portrait of Jarry.[13] In the first Surrealist Manifesto of 1924, André Breton calls Jarry a "Surrealist in absinthe" and dedicates a chapter to the latter in his *Anthology of Black Humor* (1940).[14] The resurrection from near oblivion of *Le Fond de Bain, L'Omnibus de Corinthe*, and *L'Almanach du Père Ubu* not only introduces significant, lithographic examples of turn-of-the-century art of the absurd, but, more importantly, also suggests missing links in the evolution of art of the twentieth century.

NOTES

1. Jules Roques, *Le Courrier française* (12 March 1882): 2. For a detailed discussion of the Incohérents, see L. Abélès and Cathérine Charpin, *Arts incohérents, académie du dérisoire*, catalogue of the exhibition at the Musée d'Orsay, Paris, February-May 1992.
2. *La Vie drole* was founded in 1893 by Alphonse Allais, George Auriol, and other associates of *Le Chat noir; Le Chasseur de chevelures* and *Nib* were humorous supplements to *La Revue blanche* in the early 1890s.
3. Jarry's first *Almanach du Père Ubu* of 1899 was also illustrated by Bonnard but was quite small in format and printed photomechanically. Unless otherwise stated, it is the large almanac of 1901 that is referred to in this essay.
4. For all text and images by Jarry related to Père Ubu, see *Tout Ubu*, ed. Maurice Saillet, with comments by Charles Grivel (Paris: Librairie générale française, 1985).
5. For information on Paul's life and work, see Phillip Dennis Cate and Patricia Eckert Boyer, *The Circle*

of Toulouse-Lautrec (New Brunswick, N.J.:
Zimmerli Art Museum, 1985), 112–22.

6. The possibly vulgar double entendres of the title
and of the author's name are Jarryesque in nature.

7. My thanks to the print dealers Anne and Arène
Bonafous-Murat for giving me access to their
archives related to Marc Mouclier. By coincidence,
their shop at 15 rue de l'Echaudé, Paris, was the
office of *Le Mercure de France,* which Jarry often
visited as a regular contributor to that journal.

8. See Geneviève Aitken, *Artistes et Théatres d'avant-
garde,* programmes de théatre illustrés, Paris
1890–1900, exhibition catalogue, Musée de Pully,
October 1991.

9. Emile Goudeau, "Les Grecs," *Fleurs du bitume*
(Paris: Alphonse Lemerre, 1878), 86–87.

10. For the text, which was originally published in
1918, see Guillaume Apollinaire, *Le Flaneur des
deux rives* (Paris: Gallimard, 1993), 112.

11. Antoine Terrasse, *Bonnard Illustrateur* (Paris:
Adam Biro, 1988), 60.

12. Alfred Jarry, "Minutes d'art," *Essai d'Art Libre*
(February-March-April 1894): 40.

13. For a reproduction of this drawing, now located in
the Musée Picasso, Paris, see John Richardson, *A
Life of Picasso,* vol. 1, (New York: Random House,
1991), 358.

14. André Breton, *Manifestoes of Surrealism,* trans.
Richard Seaver and Helen R. Lane (Ann Arbor:
University of Michigan Press, 1994), 27; André
Breton, *Anthologie de l'humour noir* (Paris:
Librairie générale française, 1991), 271–88.

4 | FRANK MORLEY FLETCHER AND

THE JAPANESE COLOR PRINT

NANCY E. GREEN

IN 1951 ALLAN SEABY WROTE A letter to Frank Morley Fletcher's niece Hilda describing the time he had spent with her uncle at the School of Art in Reading, England, at the end of the nineteenth century and the early part of the twentieth. He related a rather telling anecdote about the artist, describing an incident that took place "when the Japanese Exhibition was on."[1]

> In [the exhibition] was a booth where Japanese craftsmen were cutting wood blocks and printing from them. Fletcher went there with one of his prints and after watching the craftsmen—and women—at work, held out his print to their notice. The Japs [sic] examined it closely, turned it over and looked somewhat puzzled at Frank Morley Fletcher who, spare and fair haired, looked quite unlike a Jap. Then he held out his hands—you remember he had long arms and fingers and could reach across a barrier—and showed them calluses on the knuckles of his right hand

and one callus on the tip of his middle finger of his left hand. Then the craftsmen burst into smiles: they recognized him as a brother of their craft. A worker can always be known by his marks.[2]

This story fixes on what made Fletcher such a success. His English charm and obvious daring in approaching the Japanese masters are qualities that carried Fletcher through a lifetime of commitment to art and the teaching of it, and of a firm belief in art's close relationship with everyday life.

Morley Fletcher was born in Whiston, England, in 1866—the fifth of ten children. As a child in the middle, he must have felt the need to exert himself and individualize his efforts. Early on he was educated at prep school in Brighton, followed by high school at the Liverpool Institute. In 1883 he spent several months in Chênée, Belgium, learning French; this was followed by a course at University College, Liverpool, and study at the University of London. Finally, he served an apprenticeship in the engineering works in Liverpool. This endeavor undoubtedly pleased his father, who was district inspector of Alkali Works in Liverpool at the time, and later, in 1884, chief inspector in London. But his son slowly rebelled, first by studying and teaching at St. John's Wood Art School in London, then by taking classes in the studio of the Belgian painter Hubert Vos.

In 1888 Fletcher went to Paris where he spent the winter studying at the Académie Julian, followed by two years as a pupil at the Atelier Cormon, with a six-month interlude in New York. During this time, he managed to become engaged and then unengaged to a French girl. He also met the American student, Albert Herter, who would later invite him to teach in Santa Barbara.

By the early 1890s, after three years of art

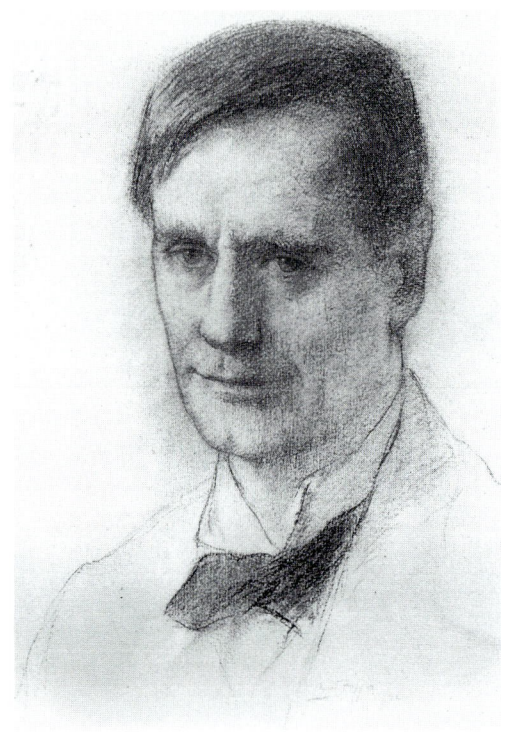

training abroad, his mind was made up. In 1894, while staying in the town of Wiston Mill, Fletcher wrote his father a letter in which his determination to be an artist had crystallized: "I wish, Father, I could persuade all of you that in spite of the little money it can make, it is work to be in earnest about and that it is worth a man's doing. If I find I cannot make enough money to live in Town then I will live most of the year away in such a place as this where I can live on very little."[3] At this time Fletcher had high hopes of making a decent living as a portrait painter, having already had several successes in this genre. He was also exhibiting in the principal London galleries and had won a medal in the British section of the World's Columbian Exhibition in Chicago in 1893 for his painting *Shadow of Death*. His high hopes seemed justified.

In 1896, while teaching at the Central School for Arts and Crafts in London,

Fletcher's career took a different turn. He had come across an article by T. Tokuno, chief of the Bureau of Engraving and Printing of the Japanese Ministry of Finance, entitled "Japanese Wood-cutting and Wood-cut Printing," first published by the Smithsonian Institution in 1893. Tokuno's article described the printing of woodcuts in color, a process popular in Japan since the 1760s when hand-colored woodcuts went out of fashion. In 1856 Felix Braquemond introduced Japanese color woodcuts to the Parisian art world, but although their influence was immediately felt in the work of the leading artists of the day, the actual making of color woodcuts in the West would take a lot longer.

In 1896, Fletcher's friend and colleague, John Dickson Batten, who had been experimenting for several years with color printing from both wood and metal blocks, printed the first British color woodcut that employed traditional Japanese methods. This print, entitled *Eve and the Serpent,* with its combination of a complex color scheme and intricate composition, seems a highly ambitious first attempt.[4] Six blocks were cut, some in cherry and some in boxwood, and one metal plate was used as a monotype plate. There were problems, not least of which were the difficulties of registration and printing. In printing an edition for the publication the *Studio,* Batten found it was easiest to reproduce the image as a chromolithograph.

The image and design for *Eve and the Serpent* were Batten's, although Fletcher provided printing skills for some of the later prints of this image. The first really collaborative effort between Batten and Fletcher occurred in 1897 when they produced *The Harpies,* also reproduced for the *Studio.* This was followed later in the same year by Fletcher's first solo effort, *Meadowsweet,* which was published by Batten in a limited

edition of seventy-five impressions. The image, a distinctly English farm and riverscape near his native Whiston, owes much in composition and feeling to the influence of Japanese art. The perspective, subtle coloration, and overall effect of calm and serenity can all be found in the art of the Japanese ukiyo-e masters. His later work would have fewer references to Japanese prints.

From the beginning, Fletcher, like his American counterpart, the art educator Arthur Wesley Dow, insisted that the Western artist should perform all aspects of the process: creating the print, drawing the design, cutting the blocks, and, finally, printing with care to register each block so the colors would be aligned. This is in contrast to the traditional Japanese manner in which each part of the process is performed by a different master artisan, with the artist serving only as the designer.

Despite using this more demanding method, Fletcher never tried to compensate by making his prints simplistic. His compositions were complex, his sense of color was sophisticated, and the end results were almost always riveting. The editions were usually between seventy-five and one hundred impressions, which probably explains why Fletcher's overall output was very small. His early prints often include a printed monogram consisting of the capital letters *M* and *F,* separated by an upward-pointing arrow. The blocks themselves were cherry wood and the colors were made of watercolor mixed with a rice-flour paste as a binder. Fletcher never used a printing press, only a hand-held baren. He was enamored of the process itself, seeing it "like an actual sketch, and in it the artist has a chance for the depiction of real life in a simple and appealing way. Woodcuts are one of the most delicate types of art, embodying soft coloring and fine lining with a

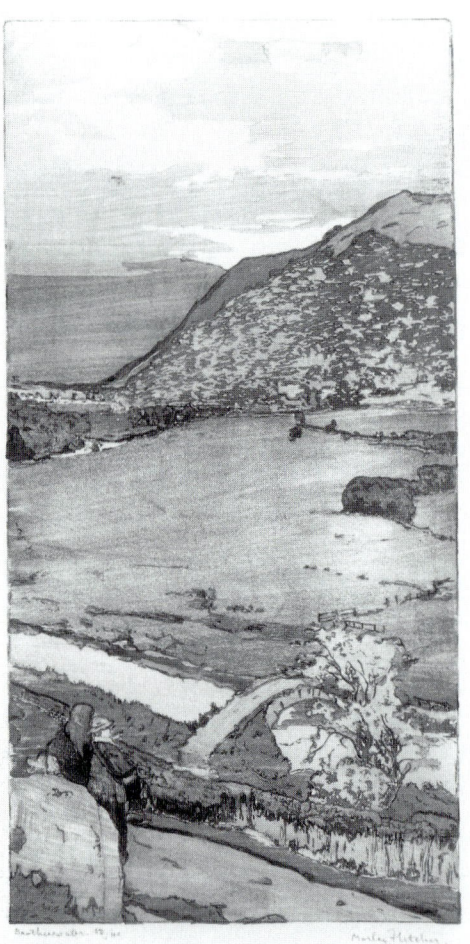

Fletcher's personal life was also changing. In 1895 he married Maud Evelyn Brown, known as Dolly, who, like Fletcher, came from a large family. Fletcher met her while on a painting trip near her family's home in Suffolk, and they seem to have enjoyed a happy relationship. She had had a career on the Lobero Stage and throughout her marriage sustained her interest in contemporary theater, often teaching drama classes. She was also a leader of the woman's suffrage movement during World War I.

This was also the beginning of Fletcher's teaching career. In 1896 he was appointed teacher of Drawing from the Life at the Central School of Arts and Crafts under the London Council and, at the same time, he inaugurated a class in the making of color prints from wood blocks using the Japanese method. On taking up teaching at University College, Reading, later that year, he continued to teach the color print class for five years. In 1898, under the direction of Walter Crane, he was appointed director at Reading. He was also curator of the Reading Corpora-

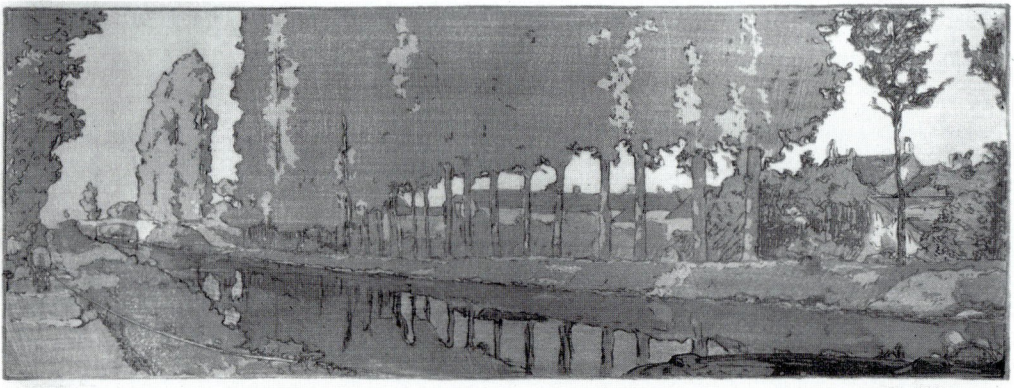

Nancy E.

Green

chance for a photographic type of reproduction, and atmospheric impression or symbolical effect. They are, in many ways a most perfect means of expression."[5]

tion Art Gallery and secretary of the Berkshire Art Society.

For the next eight years, while Fletcher was director at Reading, many students, who would become leading graphic artists both in England and abroad, came to the school to study printmaking under him. Seaby, John Platt, Ernest Lumsden, and B. J. O. Nordfeldt all studied with him here.[6] During this busy time Fletcher also pursued his own printing interests and produced several more evocative images of his native Lancashire, including *The Mountain, Brotherswater* (figure 4.2), *Lamorna, Waterway* (figure 4.3), and *Wiston River*. These prints show the power and skill of both Fletcher the artist and Fletcher the printer. The diagonal perspective pays homage to the great ukiyo-e masters—but there the similarities to Japanese color woodcuts end. The scenes are distinctly English: gently rolling hills, peaceful waterways, grazing animals, and river locks. No one would ever mistake these scenes for any place other than rural England.

The printing itself is carefully thought out and deliberate, not surprising in a man of Fletcher's temperament. Muted colors are often contrasted with saturated bright greens and turquoise; in this he paid homage to Puvis de Chavannes, the French artist Fletcher admired (above all others) for his selection of beautiful tones and colors and for the spiritual harmony found in all his works. Fletcher was also adept at *bokashi*, the careful grading of dark color to light in specific areas within the composition, such as in the changing color of the water in *Meadowsweet* and the sky in *Flood-gates* (figure 4.4). When it came to experimentation, Fletcher was not timid, and his daring shows in the resultant prints.

During this period Fletcher was also actively exhibiting his prints, drawings, and paintings. The Royal Academy, the International Society of Painters, Sculptors, and Gravers, and the South Kensington Museum (now the Victoria and Albert Museum) all hung his work. In an article published in the 11 August 1900 issue of *Black and White*, the reviewer became a quick convert to Fletcher's color prints and compared the delicacy of his woodcuts to the greatest print master of the time, James McNeill Whistler:

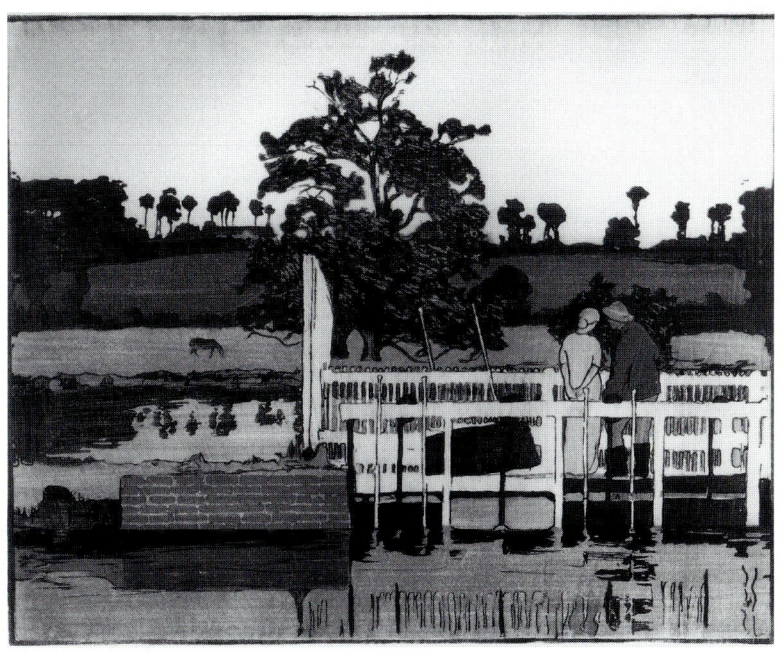

Mr. Fletcher himself is an enthusiast, and thinks that more satisfaction can be got out of a good print than out of paint pure and simple. Paint is so insufficient in form, and the line that one needs for the Japanese print pulls the picture so well together. . . . Curiously enough, this craft has played a very important part in recent developments of another fascinating form of art —namely, etching. I am speaking only from hearsay, but the tale is so good that it must be true. This Japanese plan of printing flat tones of colour seems to have caught Whistler's attention, and the extraordinary richness of some of his later etchings is due very largely to the fact that he has adapted the Japanese process to his own needs. Instead of leaving an

4.4 FRANK MORLEY FLETCHER. *Flood-gates*, 1899. Color woodcut, 20.6 x 25.6 cm. Private collection.

Frank Morley Fletcher and the Japanese Color Print

occasional tint or tone, so vital to many an etching, to the casual fancy of an art printer, Whistler carefully maps out the spots where the tone is to fall, and with the Japanese woodcut lays a sort of ground for the later impression from the copper.[7]

Many artists, like Whistler, had been greatly enamored of the ukiyo-e prints, but the actual use of the color woodcut medium in the West awaited such artists as Batten and Fletcher. Also at this time, Fletcher was a member of the Council of the International Society of Sculptors, Painters, and Gravers, and he organized several art shows, including the 1906 Whistler Memorial Exhibition.

In 1906 Fletcher reluctantly accepted an appointment working for the Board of Education as inspector of art schools in the southeast and southwest districts of England. He did not enjoy this job, probably because the administrative duties left little time for his real mission of educating. In 1908, when the opportunity arose to become the first director of the newly established Edinburgh College of Art, he was more than happy to make the move northward.

In an article written about Fletcher soon after he took the Edinburgh job, he was said to have "a quiet, unassuming nature. . . . [He] has a most engaging personality, and is a fascinating conversationalist to those who have the privilege of his acquaintance. He is an accomplished archaeologist, dearly loves his morning canter in the saddle, nor is he above putting on the gloves now and then to satisfy those of his students who are intrepid enough to meet him in a friendly bout."[8] This quick study seems an apt picture of Fletcher as he entered midcareer.

By this time Fletcher's color woodcuts had been purchased for the South Kensington Museum, galleries in Dresden and Budapest,

and the United States National Museum.[9] His reputation was growing and he was able to attract a number of preeminent artists to the college as lecturers, including Walter Crane, D. Y. Cameron, William Strang, and C. F. A. Voysey. Another guest lecturer was Joseph Pennell, "who always spoke his mind, scarcely even preserving the `gentle art of making enemies.'" Despite his lifelong advocacy of Whistler as the unrivaled artist-printmaker, Pennell did admit of Fletcher that "he has not in any way tried to imitate the Japanese subjects or to make copies of them, but he has carried out the feeling of the English country and of other European countries in his color prints, made as the Japanese make their prints."[10] J. Craig Annan also lectured at the college on "artistic expression in photography," showing Fletcher's openness to newer media and their importance to the changing art world.

Like many of the leading art schools of the day, the Edinburgh College of Art offered practical courses in all forms of fine and decorative arts including embroidery, architecture, house painting, animal study, book illustration, stained glass, furniture and dress design, book finishing, leather tooling, repoussé work, and chasing. The color woodcut course was also of a practical nature, offered in cooperation with the printing department of Heriot-Watt College. This course examined drawing and design for the special purpose of advertisements, poster-work, and block printing.

The war years also proved extremely busy for Fletcher. In 1916 his manual *Wood-block Printing* was published by John Hogg. Just as Dow's book *Composition*, first published in 1899, became *the* manual that influenced a generation of American art students, Fletcher's book guided English art students in the elements of good woodcut design.

In 1916 Fletcher became involved in the work of the Design and Industries Association. This group "looked ahead to the days when the war would be over and Britain, instead of fighting the Germans, would be competing with them in the market for manufactured goods. The directors of the association realized the very close connection between the design of the article (furniture, clothing, household equipment, for example) and its sales value."[11] The aim of the association was "fitness for purpose," emphasizing sound materials and honest workmanship. The idea, rather like those of William Morris in concept, was not a new one. But unlike Morris and his circle, the association accepted and condoned manufactured articles, if they were well made. The social side to this was the real attraction for Fletcher—that quality of work could improve life for the laborers by giving them pride in their work and result in beautifully produced articles for everyday use.

In 1917 Fletcher participated in a program developed by English universities to send experts on various subjects to the war zone to provide educational lectures to the men in the ranks. In his talks, Fletcher set forth the ideas of the Design and Industries Association, stressing quality in work and a particular need for pride in one's work if it was to be done well. He also sought to "disabuse the minds of his audiences of any conception of art as something merely ornamental and extraneous to practical life."[12] It is hard to know exactly what the soldiers actually thought of these talks, but Fletcher was pleased with his reception and found a surprisingly keen interest in art among these men.

One of the loveliest of Fletcher's prints, *The Bookworm* (figure 4.5), was probably produced around this time.[13] This is a portrait of Maud's sister Emma, who married one of Fletcher's painter friends, Walter Cadby. It is

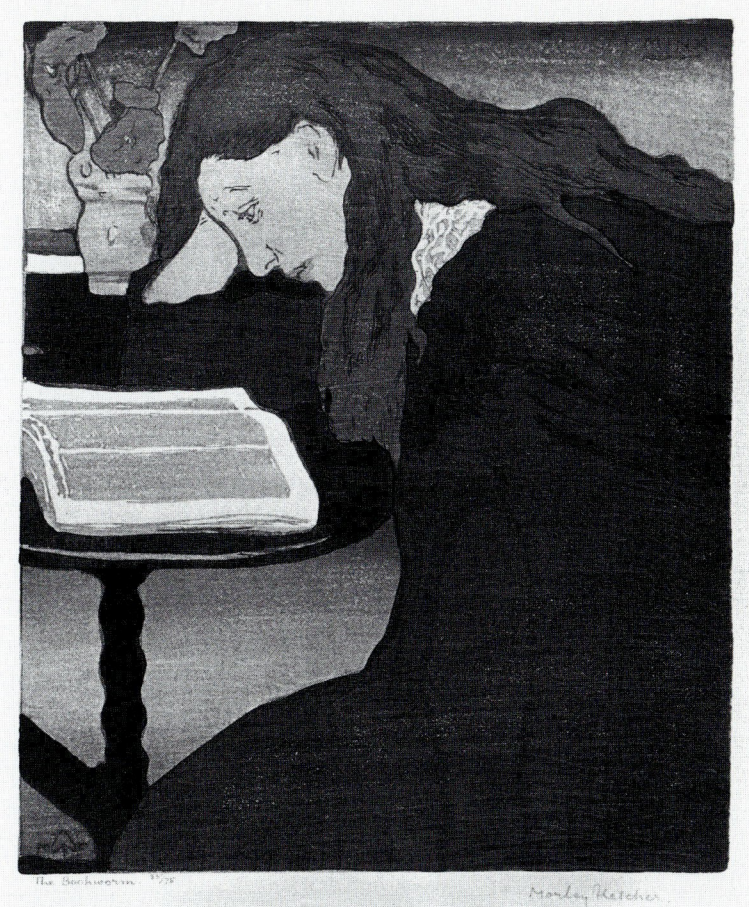

Fletcher's only portrait print and shows a daydreaming figure bent over her book. The immediacy of the figure pressed against the picture frame intimately involves the viewer in the woman's reverie. This print is sometimes referred to as *The Blue Girl* because of the color of her dress, although Fletcher experimented with printing the image in both red and green. Certainly one of the most decorative prints produced by the artist, it was popular from the beginning.

Several of Fletcher's former students came to Edinburgh in the teens and early twenties to join the teaching staff there. Ernest Lumsden taught at the new school, alongside the color woodcut artist Mabel Royds, who would

4.5 FRANK MORLEY FLETCHER. *The Bookworm*, 1920–23. Color woodcut, 23.5 x 21 cm. Collection, San Diego Museum of Art, gift of the University Women's Club.

Frank Morley Fletcher and the Japanese Color Print

become his wife in 1913. They spent their honeymoon traveling widely and many of Royds's prints are images of India where they lived during most of World War I. In 1918 she was back in Edinburgh, teaching again at

This enthusiasm for the color print in California may have been the reason Fletcher was first invited to come visit and lecture in the Santa Barbara area in 1923. Fletcher's old friend Albert Herter made all the arrange-

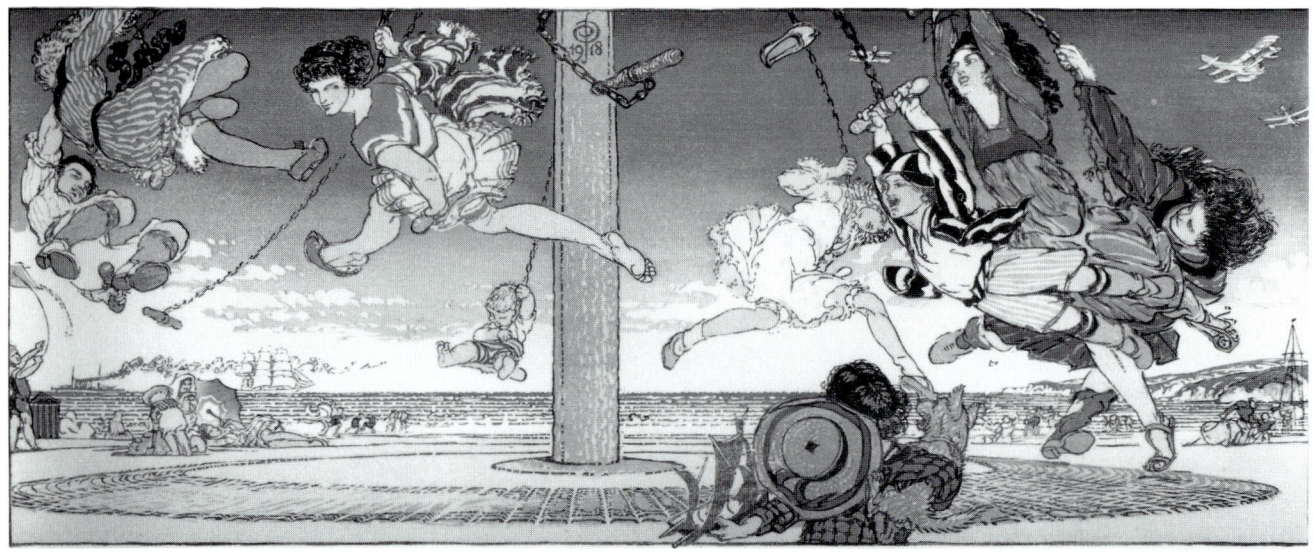

4.6 JOHN PLATT. *The Giant Stride*, 1918, color woodcut, 14.2 x 41 cm. Collection, Herbert F. Johnson Museum of Art, Cornell University, purchased with funds donated by Phyllis Goody Cohen, class of 1956.

the college where she eventually took over Fletcher's wood-cutting and wood-block printing class when he moved to America in 1923.

John Platt also came to Edinburgh to teach in the early 1920s. Platt had made great progress as a woodcut artist since his student days in Reading. His print *The Giant Stride* (figure 4.6) is an important step beyond Fletcher's teaching to a more modern image that encompasses the idea of motion as part of the composition. This transition to an untraditional subject marked a distinct change in the newer, Western woodcuts, which no longer seemed tied to the theme of landscape commonly associated with ukiyo-e prints. *The Giant Stride* was awarded the gold medal when it was shown in Los Angeles at the International Exhibition organized by the Society of California Printmakers in 1922, and in 1925 it won the Storrow Prize for the best color woodcut.[14]

ments, setting up lectures and social gatherings so the Fletchers could easily become acquainted with the area. They also took a six-month tour of America, visiting art schools throughout the country, while Maud gave a number of Shakespearean recitals. By the time Fletcher returned to Edinburgh, he had been offered the directorship of the Santa Barbara School of the Arts.

In 1923 Fletcher was near retirement. After fifteen years at Edinburgh he had built up his pension and could look forward to receiving it in a few years time. But he was restless. As he wrote to his mother, soon after his return from the United States, "In Edinburgh for two years I have felt that the maximum of work I can do for the college has been done and I would rather not sit waiting for a very small pension. So I am very thankful for the new enterprise and for pioneer work again. I have written explaining matters to the chairman of my Board at the college."[15]

On 10 October 1923, the *Scotsman* reported his resignation.

But it wasn't just the new challenge. California provided opportunities for Maud as well and the attraction of the beautiful climate and good friends was too much for the couple to resist. From the start Fletcher was pleased with the enthusiasm he found there. Again, he offered classes in graphic design and woodblock printing and, over the next few years, invited his artist friends, such as Charles Paine, William Bagdatopoulos, and Franz Geritz, to teach or lecture at the new school. He enlarged the curriculum to include drawing, painting from life, color study, outdoor painting, decorative design, sculpture, architectural design, drama study, voice, production, harmony, singing, piano, ballet, social dancing, and French. Maud taught classes as well, in the study and reading of contemporary drama. In this way, Fletcher established Santa Barbara as an active arts center in the 1920s.

He began to cut blocks in the winter of 1927 for his first major American print, *California 1: Salinas River* (figure 4.7). It is a magnificent view with a dazzling vista showing the swath of the Salinas River flowing majestically across the sheet. Whatever else California meant to Fletcher, the print shows a respect and appreciation for the great American vista and an obvious love of his adopted country. The Fletchers also enticed family members to come and stay. Maud's sisters Elsie and Gladys both moved to California with their families. America seemed to offer all the opportunities they needed; in 1926, Fletcher became a naturalized citizen.

When the depression hit, the Santa Barbara School of Art came to an untimely end. The next few years were hard ones, although Fletcher used the time creatively. In 1929 he was named vice president of the Printmakers Society of California and soon thereafter

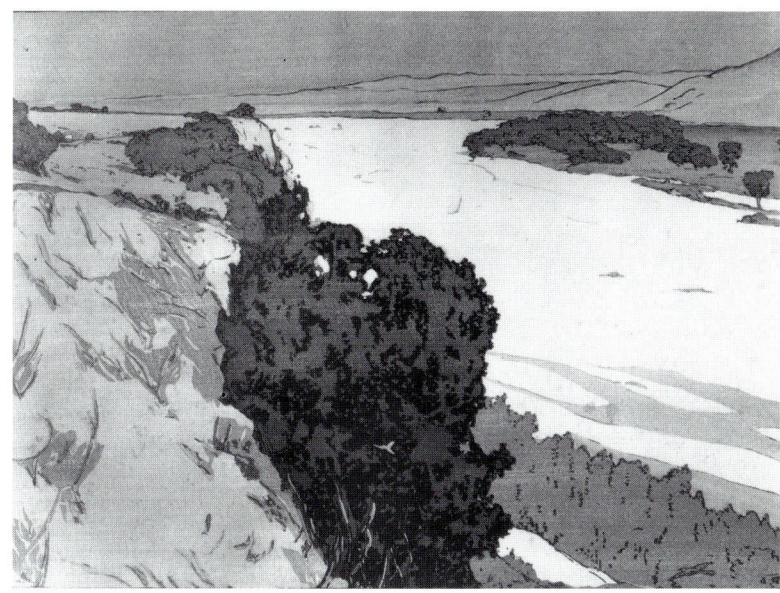

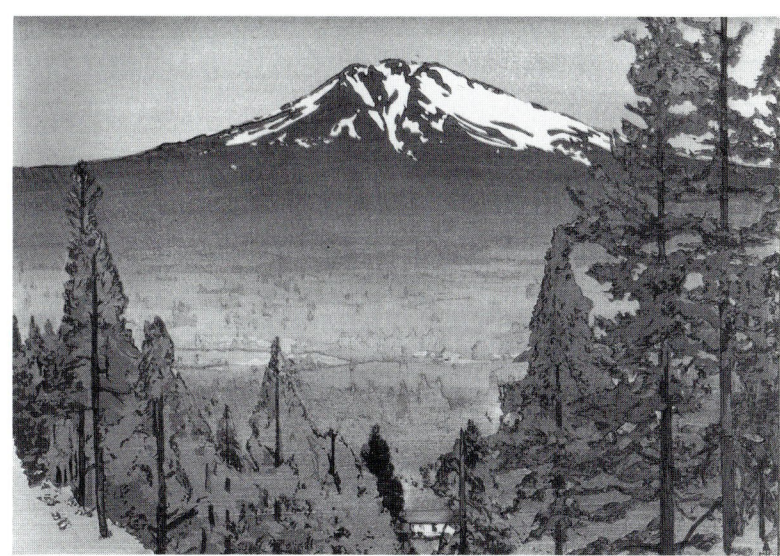

4.7 FRANK MORLEY FLETCHER. *California 1: Salinas River*, 1927–28. Color woodcut, 32.3 x 43.2 cm. Private collection.

4.8 FRANK MORLEY FLETCHER. *Mount Shasta*, 1932. Color woodcut, 28.8 x 40.6 cm. Collection, The Fine Arts Museums of San Francisco, Achenbach Foundation for Graphic Arts, gift of Mr. and Mrs. F. A. Lejeune.

began work on his second western print, *California 2: Mount Shasta* (figure 4.8). This image bears the closest resemblance of any of Fletcher's prints to his spiritual mentor, Hokusai. Like Mount Fuji, Mount Shasta

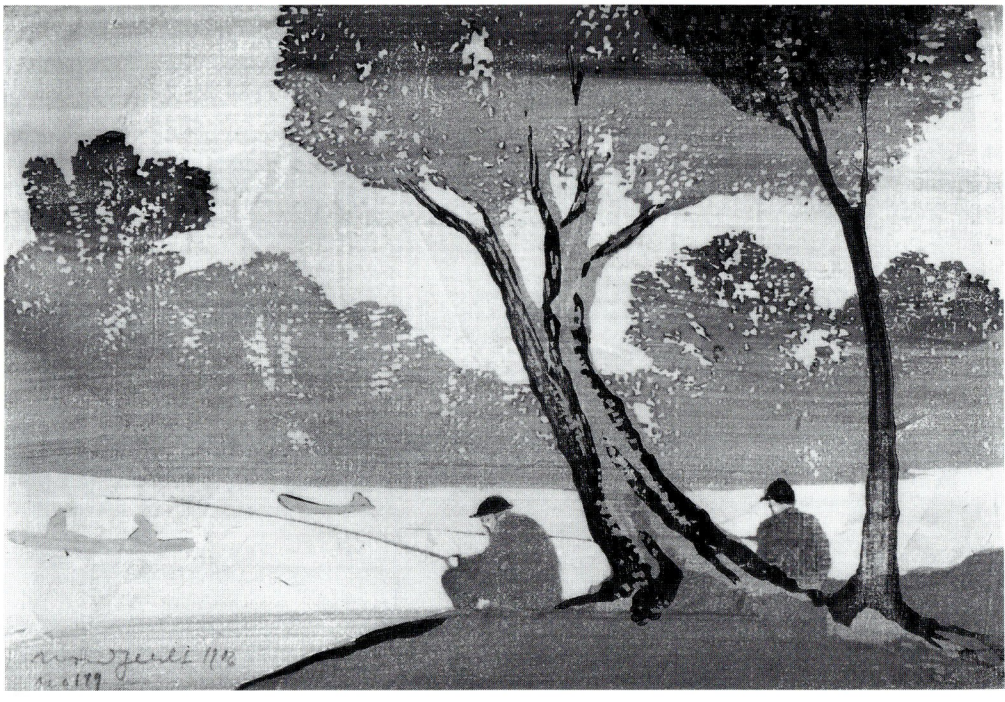

rises triumphantly at the center of the composition and represents the best of Fletcher's design and printing skills. The mountainous landscape seems to have fully captured the artist's heart and imagination, and the result pays homage to the grandeur of an awe-inspiring view.

Fletcher's prints were now being shown regularly in exhibitions around the country. His sensitivity to the woodcut medium was appreciated by reviewers and the general public alike. Reginald Poland, a frequent reviewer for the *San Diego Sun* and director of the Fine Arts Gallery of San Diego, always spoke favorably of the artist. In a 1931 article, he noted that in his prints Fletcher "tries to suggest the spirit, beauty and character of the subject in a still more artistic pattern than might be possible with merely a photographic representation of the physical world."[16] In 1932 his entire oeuvre to date—thirteen prints—was shown at the Leggett Studios in New York.[17] This consisted of *Meadowsweet,*

Flood-gates, Brotherswater, Wiston River, The Mountain, Lamorna, The Avenue, Waterway, Tre'pied, The Bookworm, California 1: Salinas River, California 2: Mount Shasta, and *Pilgrimage Play,* a print Fletcher produced in collaboration with the artist Allen Tierney. His last print, *Ojai Valley,* was completed around 1935.

In the early thirties the Fletchers moved for a short while to Los Angeles, where Fletcher tried to revive his career as a portrait painter. In 1934 he opened an art clinic that offered advice and aid to students or anyone who needed assistance in the arts. Many artists offered their services at the clinic including Carl Oscar Borg, Paul Landacre, and Millard Sheets. The same year there was also a well-received show of Fletcher's work and the work of his students at the Division of Graphic Arts, Smithsonian Institution. And Fletcher continued to lecture wherever he was invited.

The Fletchers returned to Ojai in the mid-

1930s. Fletcher's eyesight had begun to cause him problems and after completing *Ojai Valley* he made no more color woodcuts. He did continue to paint and write, however, and in 1936 his book *Color Control* was published by Faber and Faber, London. In this slim volume he divulged a system he had worked out while director of the Edinburgh College of Art with which artists could organize their palettes in terms of color intervals rather than by the more commonly followed sequence of particular color pigments.

Fletcher continued to work and paint throughout the forties, occasionally taking in a private student, but finally just enjoying his last years in the coastal country he had grown to love. He and his wife died in 1949, but his legacy of teaching and sharing with so many others his strong love for art remained. He would be remembered for his beautiful color woodcuts and his enthusiasm in bringing to both English and American artists the joys of the Japanese technique. Today his prints and original wood blocks are in many public and private collections, including, in Britain, the British Museum and Victoria and Albert Museum, London; the Hunterian Art Gallery, Glasgow; and, in the United States, the Boston Museum of Fine Arts; Smithsonian Institution; San Diego Museum of Art; Santa Barbara Museum of Art; and the Fine Arts Museums of San Francisco, Achenbach Foundation for Graphic Arts.

NOTES

1. This would probably have been in 1898 during the World's Fair in London. Fletcher, along with several other English printmakers, studied with the visiting Japanese printers and learned to produce multicolored woodcuts. Fletcher had his Japanese tools, brushes, and colors duplicated by English craftsmen. The rest of the necessary materials— papers, bamboo leaf, barens, and inks—were imported from Japan.

2. Allan W. Seaby to Hilda Morley Fletcher, 29 April 1951, private collection.

3. Frank Morley Fletcher to his father, Alfred Evans Fletcher, 14 September 1894, private collection.

4. In a letter to the *Studio* (vol. 7, 1896), Batten describes his process. He sized Japanese paper with milk; his paints consisted of powdered pigments ground with a mixture of dextrine and glycerines. Batten does not mention Fletcher in this article, but mentions a Mr. Ellingham as having cut two of the blocks for *Eve and the Serpent.* Batten painstakingly printed several impressions at this time. In an 1897 letter to the *Studio* (vol. 10), Batten describes further experiments. By this time he has consulted Fletcher about the printing of both the *Eve* print and a new image called *The Harpies.* The milk sizing and glycerine and dextrine mixture were abandoned. The impression of *Eve and the Serpent* owned by the Hunterian Art Gallery, Glasgow, was probably made at this time; Batten signed and numbered the print "No. 42"; "Printed by F. Morley Fletcher" is written in Fletcher's hand.

5. "Field of Art Unsettled Like Rest of World Today, Says Frank Morley Fletcher," *Santa Barbara Daily News,* 1 August 1931.

6. For Nordfeldt, who occupies a central position in the history of the color woodcut in the United States, see Fiona Donavan, *The Woodblock Prints of B.J.O. Nordfeldt,* (Minneapolis: University Art Museum, University of Minnesota, 1991). During study at the Art Institute of Chicago, Nordfeldt's work attracted the attention of visiting muralist Albert Herter, Fletcher's friend from their school days in Paris. Herter invited Nordfeldt to assist him with a mural commission for the Paris Exposition in 1900. After a period of work in Paris, Nordfeldt studied at Reading under Fletcher, whom he may have heard of through Herter. Nordfeldt's earliest color prints, such as *Two Fishermen* (figure 4.9), were strongly influenced by the Japanese ukiyo-e masters.

7. "The Japanese and Ourselves: How Their Craft Influences Our Art," *Black and White,* 11 August 1900.

8. "F. Morley Fletcher, Esq.," *Gazetteer,* 16 June 1910.

9. The South Kensington Museum is now the Victoria and Albert Museum; the United States National

Museum was part of the Smithsonian Institution.

10. Pennell, quoted in Reginald Poland, "Art Gallery Topics," *San Diego Sun*, n.d. (ca. 1933–34).

11. Arnold and Gladys Lejeune, "Woodblock Printing in Santa Barbara," *Noticias*, Santa Barbara Historical Society, n.p., n.d.

12. "Art and War: Scottish Visit to France," *Scotsman*, 3 April 1917.

13. Many of Fletcher's prints are not dated, and it is difficult to pinpoint the exact year in which they were completed. Also, editions were not always printed all at once and there might be a significant time lapse between printings. *The Bookworm* was probably conceived in the late teens or early twenties and is a portrait of Maud's sister Emma, who married the artist Walter Cadby, a friend of Fletcher's from his student days. Emma was the only one of Maud's three sisters who did not move to America soon after the Fletchers, in 1923. Although he could have produced this from a photograph, it is likelier that Fletcher made this woodcut before moving to California, thus dating it between 1920 and 1923.

14. In a 1925 article for the *Studio* (vol. 90, p. 293), Platt describes the appeal of the woodcut for modern printmakers: "Woodblock colour printing compels clear thinking about pictorial construction, because the lines and the masses printed from woodblocks are necessarily precise and definite. This medium necessitates selection and elimination, the expression of the idea stripped of its very nature makes the artist aim for an abstraction rather than a literal rendering of nature."

15. Fletcher to his mother, Sarah Morley Fletcher, 3 September 1923, private collection.

16. Reginald Poland, "Woodblocks by Fletcher Hold Interest," *San Diego Sun*, 3 October 1931.

17. A 1905 flyer advertising Fletcher's print *Brotherswater* mentions four other prints, including one called *Minx*. I have not seen such a print; it has been neither mentioned nor illustrated in any other listing of the artist's work.

5 | THE CASE OF
Childe Hassam's Lithographs
THE ABSENT PRINTER

CLINTON ADAMS

IN 1980, WHILE DISCUSSING LITHO-graphic techniques and the abilities of printers in an early draft of *American Lithographers, 1900–1960,* I wrote: "Although many artists have believed that [the New York printer, George C.] Miller discouraged artists from use of tusche washes, suggestions that he did so because he was unskilled in printing such washes are quickly refuted through examination of the superb wash lithographs that Miller printed for Childe Hassam in 1918."[1]

There are five such lithotints—as Hassam preferred to call them—each impressive in its own way. Hassam's sparkling washes in *The Lithographer* (figure 5.1), *Lafayette Street* (figure 5.2), and *The French Cruiser* (figure 5.3) are fearlessly drawn, "like the stroke of a disciplined oar,"[2] and demonstrate a painterly command of the medium unequalled in American lithography of the time. The deceptively simple composition of *Lafayette Street* is, in fact, quite adventurous. Split sharply down the center, the rigid geometry of the

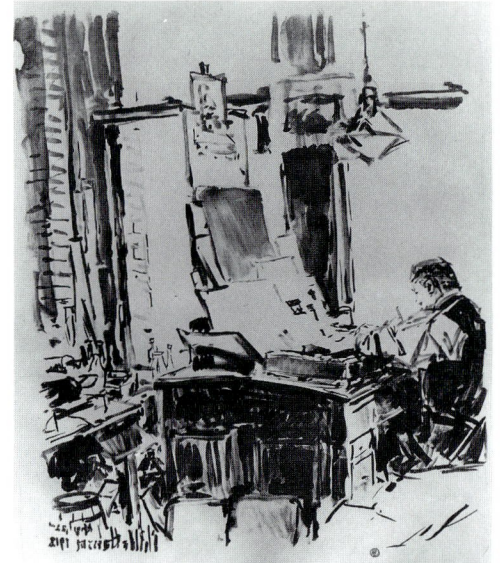

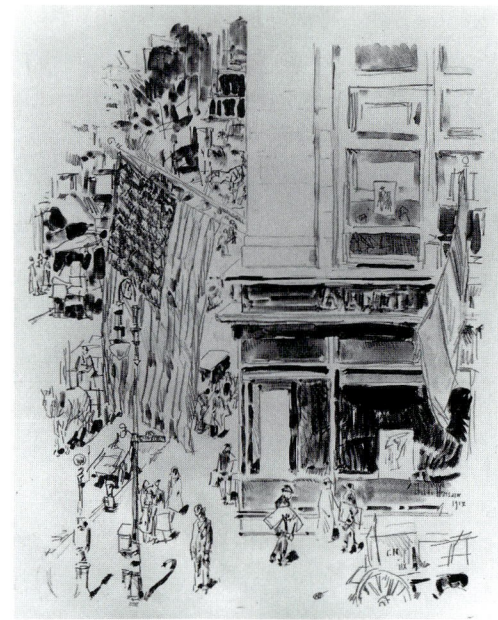

5.1 CHILDE HASSAM. *The Lithographer* (Griffith 9), 1918. Wash lithograph, 45.1 x 30.9 cm (sheet). Collection, Worcester Art Museum, gift of Mrs. Childe Hassam (1940.21.10).

5.2 CHILDE HASSAM. *Lafayette Street* (Griffith 5), 1918. Wash lithograph, 45.3 x 29.3 cm (sheet). Collection, Worcester Art Museum, gift of Mrs. Childe Hassam (1940.21.11).

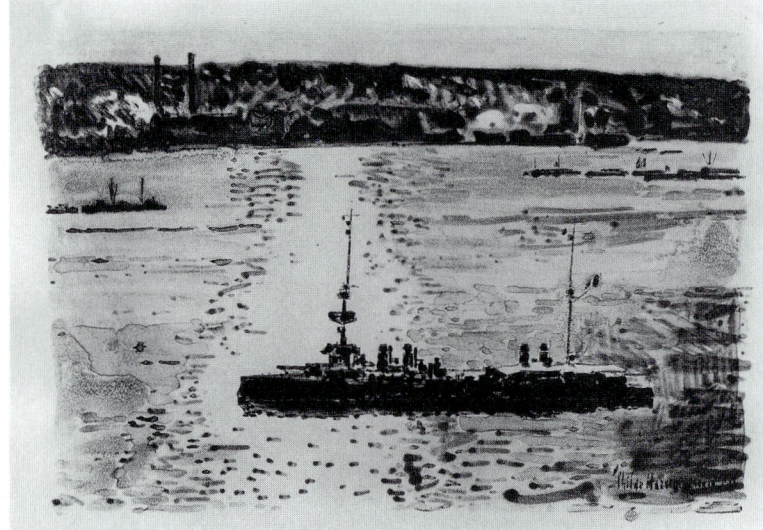

5.3 CHILDE HASSAM. *French Cruiser* (Griffith 13), 1918. Wash lithograph, 29.4 x 45.3 cm (sheet). Collection, Worcester Art Museum, gift of Mrs. Childe Hassam (1940.21.18).

building, drawn partially in crayon, plays against the loosely interwoven complexity of the busy avenue and flag, sketched in a Fauvist shorthand. With similar daring, Hassam creates in *The French Cruiser* a small masterpiece of Impressionist printmaking, boldly silhouetting the black shapes of the ships and distant shore against the blinding light of river and sky. By contrast, *The Broad Curtain* (figure 5.4), an intimate interior reminiscent of Bonnard and Vuillard,

is a study in light, filtering through the curtain and illuminating the figure of Mrs. Hassam, who sits knitting in her chair. *Storm King* (figure 5.5) is far more abstract—a brilliant tour de force in which a fluid sky hovers above the brooding mountain, the space masterfully defined by near and distant ships that float in stark white water.

There was (it then seemed) ample evidence that Miller printed these remarkable images. The historical circumstances were right. Hassam had many associations with the group of artists who on 9 January 1917 assembled in Albert Sterner's studio and, after some discussion, formed a new organization, the Painter-Gravers of America.[3] Among the artists were Sterner, George Bellows, Boardman Robinson, and John Sloan, all of whom had made lithographs. Hassam, already highly regarded as an etcher, was a charter member of the group.

Sterner had been working for several years with George Miller, who was then employed by the American Lithographic Company, but who after-hours printed stones not only for Sterner but also for Bellows and Joseph Pennell.[4] At some point early in 1917 —shortly after the formation of the Painter-Gravers of America—Miller came to believe that he might be able to make a living as a printer for artists. Gambling on this prospect, he opened a small workshop on Manhattan's Lower East Side. Childe Hassam was guided to Miller's workshop by Sterner or Pennell, where Miller printed the artist's first lithograph, *North River* [Griffith 1], a drawing on transfer paper, in the spring or early summer of 1917.

The standard reference on Hassam's lithographs is a catalogue compiled by Fuller Griffith, then associate curator of Graphic Arts at the Museum of History and Technology, a division of the Smithsonian Institution.[5] In that catalogue, first published in 1962 and reprinted in 1980, Griffith stated unequivocally that Miller printed all of Hassam's lithographs. The credibility of this statement was enhanced by Griffith's apparent communication with Miller, to whom he expressed appreciation for information about the prints.

Further evidence of Miller's role as Hassam's printer was provided through inclusion of *The Lithographer* and *The Broad Curtain* in a 1976 exhibition, "George Miller and American Lithography," organized by Janet A. Flint at the National Collection of Fine Arts (now the National Museum of American Art, also a division of the Smithsonian Institution). Hassam's name was on Miller's list, "Artists for Whom I Have Printed." When in 1934 Miller found it necessary to sell some of his printer's proofs at auction, a Hassam lithograph was included in the sale.[6]

It all seemed to fit. But then, while I was still revising the text of *American Lithographers*, Janet Flint—to whom I am greatly indebted—sent me photocopies of some sur-

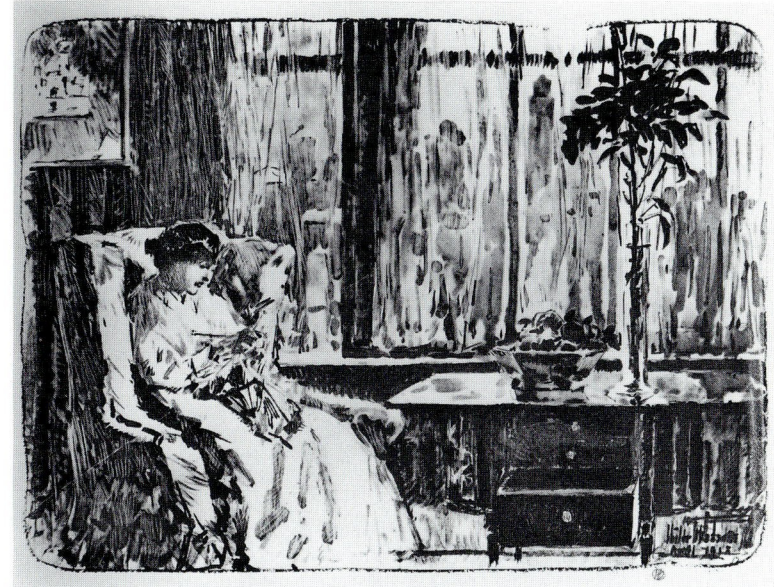

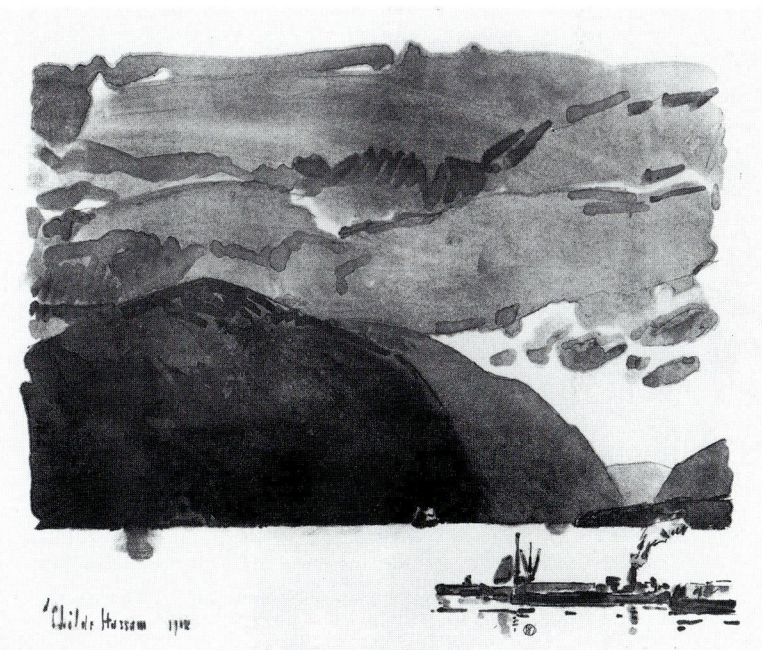

5.4 CHILDE HASSAM. *The Broad Curtain* (Griffith 29), 1918. Wash lithograph, 32.3 x 45 cm (sheet). Collection, University Art Museum, University of New Mexico (68.152).

5.5 CHILDE HASSAM. *Storm King* (Griffith 45), 1918. Wash lithograph, 29.0 x 45.5 cm (sheet). Collection, Worcester Art Museum, gift of Mrs. Childe Hassam (1940.21.29).

prising pages that were part of an unpublished manuscript, hand-written by Childe Hassam, in which he describes the making of his prints. (For clarity, I have added punctuation but have not otherwise changed Hassam's text.)

My lithotints of "the Lithographer," "Lafayette Street, New York," "La Gloire," the French cruiser that was stationed in the Hudson opposite and above 72nd Street during the war, I made directly on the stone in the shop of the commercial lithographers Oberly and Newell on Lafayette Street,[7] the oldest and most expert of their workmen being assigned to me to go through the perfectly mechanical and simple operation of treating the stone in the usual way after the drawing had been made on it; this you may do with a lithographic crayon, a pen such as I am writing with, charged with lithographic ink, or use a brush and lay water color washes just as you would on Whatman paper, merely using turpentine and lithographic printing ink; you will find it always expedient to have your washes mixed and kept stirred up well by an assistant as the ink is bound to stay at the bottom of your small bottle with its wide neck. I take pains to write this out carefully and to interpolate it here as I have never seen anywhere, even in the books that are supposed to tell you how to make a lithograph—and a lithotint—a correct description of the process. Moreover, the grey-haired expert lithographers at Oberly and Newell's said that it could not be done—Herr Faust—it was during the war and the flags of the allies were conspicuously displayed as you see in my lithotint of Lafayette Street, 1918. The answer was to Herr Faust the quick sketch of a commercial lithographer working at his bench, where the only thing that I for-

got was to reverse my signature as I had learned to do in drawing on boxwood in 1878—``The Lithographer" was done to prove to a German lithographer who must have been, if he was sixty-five then, been [sic] working at his trade since he was an apprentice in Germany at the age of fifteen, or just fifty years.

Herr Faust with his fine German name was—when he had treated the stone just as he would have done if I had used only the conventional lithographers crayon—dumbfounded. I then made the "Lafayette Street" out of the window using the lithographic crayon and the wash and you may see where the wash has curdled, as certain color pigments will do on paper; if you can give me a better word I will use it—if to curdle is to slightly separate (apart from any well defined chemical change), the pigment separates into quite well defined dots; in the case of the ink it is easily noticable [sic] in "La Gloire" [The French Cruiser] in the lower corner of the drawing, where it is very apparent. I observed to Mr. Faust who spoke En[glish] and understood it perfectly that Mr. Whistler had used the method delightfully and that, though his lithographs were never as well known as his etchings, that undoubtedly these were in some of the fine collections all over the world and even in all the countries then at war, for instance—at least some of his lithographs if not his lithotints. You may be surprised that a man from the country of Senefelder should not know one of the processes of lithography, as perhaps you are more surprised, being in a commercial establishment, that he should have known about Whistler, but he did, and I think that he knew Pennell, who was doing his lithographs of "Work" at about this time.[8]

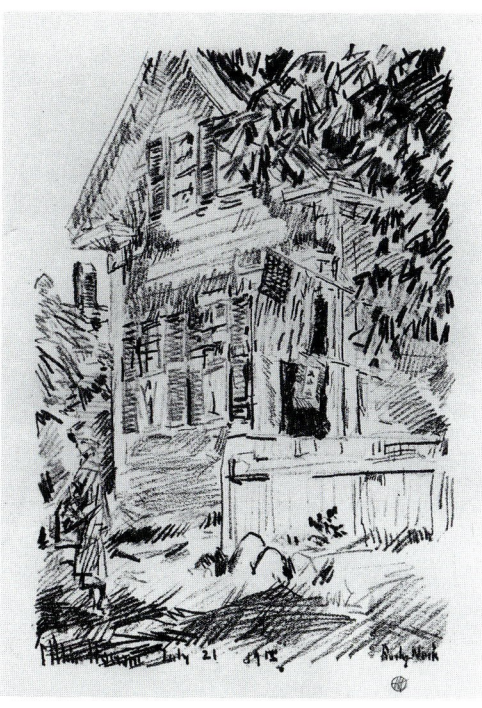

Miller's skill as a printer of tusche washes. And given that Griffith was wrong about the lithotints, might he also be wrong about the transfers? I looked at Hassam's lithograph *Portrait of Joseph Pennell* [Griffith 3] with new doubt. I had always found it hard to envision the circumstances in which Hassam, after making a drawing of Pennell at his press, might have taken it to Miller to be printed. Could Pennell himself have accomplished the transfer and printed the lithograph, I wondered?

Fortunately, I had time, before *American Lithographers* went to press, to identify "Herr Faust" as the printer of Hassam's lithotints, and to revise the caption of the Pennell portrait to read "printer unknown." In a note, I chanced a comment that it did "not have the look of Miller's printing." In 1988, five years after publication of *American Lithographers,* I returned to the Hassam puzzle, and again studied the transfer lithographs.[9] There are forty in all. Three were made in 1917; seven (by Griffith's count) were made early in 1918, either before or during the months of April and May, while Hassam worked with Faust at Oberly and Newell. Hassam then went to Gloucester, Massachusetts, where between June and September he completed (again by Griffith's count) twenty-eight drawings for subsequent transfer to plates or stones.

The Gloucester prints are remarkably diverse in execution. In some, Hassam remains an Impressionist, using his crayon to develop a radiant world of light and tone; in others he slashes his crayon across the paper with expressionistic force. Most remarkable of these "fearless, brusque notations" are *The Service Flag* (figure 5.6) and *Nude* (figure 5.7), the latter described by Elisabeth Cary as "one powerful little nude, seen from the back, and half buried in foliage indicated by broad im-

5.6 CHILDE HASSAM. *The Service Flag* (Griffith 24), 1918. Transfer lithograph, 28.7 x 22.3 (sheet). Collection, Worcester Art Museum, gift of Mrs. Childe Hassam (1940.21.6).

5.7 CHILDE HASSAM. *Nude* (Griffith 38), 1918. Transfer lithograph, 43.5 x 28.7 cm (sheet). Collection, Worcester Art Museum, gift of Mrs. Childe Hassam (1940.21.1).

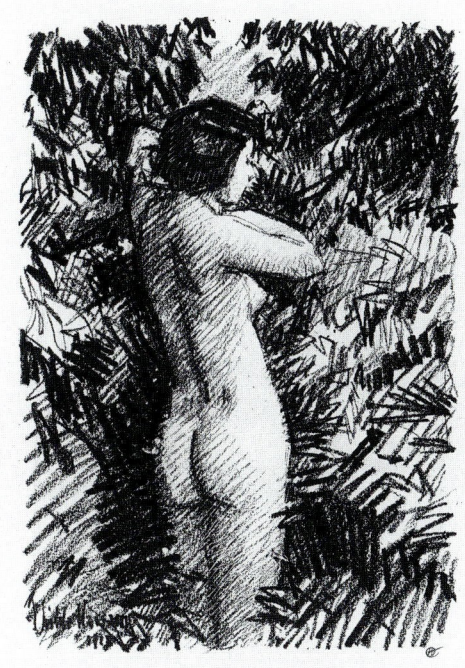

All must now be rethought. Griffith was wrong; Miller did not print Hassam's lithotints, and they thus have no relevance to

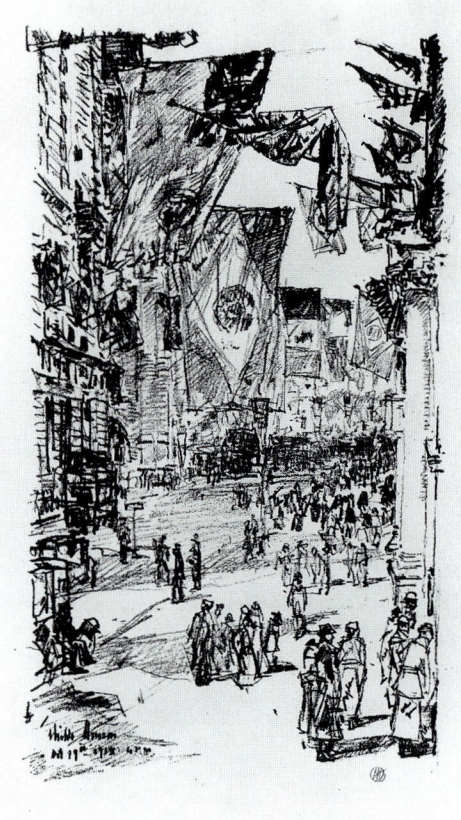

petuous lines, . . . light and shadow dappling the figure with as certain an evocation of sunlight as any created by the short brisk lines of his etchings."[10]

In lithographs such as *The Service Flag, Nude,* and *Avenue of the Allies* (figure 5.8), as in the lithotint *Storm King,* Hassam reveals a persistence of the adventurous spirit that had characterized his painting of the 1890s. It is as if lithography, particularly transfer lithography—a medium whose impromptu character encouraged improvisation—had become the catalyst through which Hassam was able to overcome the conservative spirit of his later years. By contrast with Hassam's painted "nudes in nature," in which the academic classicism of the figure is so often at odds with its Impressionist environment, the lithograph of that subject is totally convincing. In *Nude,* more than in any other work,

Hassam moves—perhaps only momentarily, but with full intensity—toward acceptance of the Fauvist and Expressionist aesthetic, both in form and spirit.[11]

When drawing on transfer paper, Hassam took full advantage of the rich effects made possible through frottage. In *Landscape, Land of Nod* [Griffith 21], the broken texture of his crayon strokes reflects the pebbled surface that he placed beneath the paper; in other prints, particularly those drawn with harder crayons, the texture is smoother, the forms more clearly defined. Close examination of the prints reveals that Hassam occasionally made minor changes in drawings after their transfer to a stone or plate. He frequently scratched white lines into dark tones with a needle or stylus; he sometimes reinforced crayon lines or tones that appeared too weak after transfer. In *Inner Harbor* [Griffith 16], he added the pale clouds on the stone or plate. (The New York Public Library has a trial proof of this image with an annotation by Hassam, "only proof without clouds.") Such changes demonstrate that Hassam was often present in the lithography workshop when the transfer drawings were proofed and printed. Working with his printer, he almost certainly determined the character of the inks used in printing, which vary from black to semitransparent black, and from warm black to brown. Unless Hassam found a qualified printer in Massachusetts (there is no evidence of this), we must assume that the lithographs drawn in Gloucester during the summer of 1918 were not printed until the artist returned to New York City in the fall of that year.

Hassam's lithographs (both lithotints and transfers) are most frequently printed on a cream wove paper, probably oriental in origin, but of a character that closely resembles papers made in France. The full sheets of this deckle-edged paper carry a distinctive watermark of a stylized paulownia (or *kiri*) flower.[12] Many of Hassam's lithographs are printed on a partial sheet of this paper, cut on one edge but retaining three deckles; as a result, the watermark does not appear on all impressions. Hassam did not use this watermarked paper for all his lithographs; within editions it is not uncommon to find variant impressions printed on other papers, sometimes on old laid papers or on the back of old engravings.[13] As Hassam printed some of his etchings on the same watermarked paper, we must conclude that it was he who supplied it to his printers—to Miller, who printed *North River*, and to Faust, who printed the lithotints—and, further, that the choice of paper provides no clue as to the identity of the printer.

The question remained: Could Miller have printed the transfer lithographs? The answer was at hand all along, startlingly obvious, but unseen by Griffith. In August 1917, only months after Miller opened his workshop, the United States entered World War I; soon thereafter, Miller, who was by avocation a fervent sailor, enlisted in the navy. To confirm the dates of Miller's military service, I wrote to his son Burr.

I know that he enlisted as soon as war was declared [Burr Miller replied]. . . . The Navy was so hard up for experienced mechanics that he didn't even go to boot camp. . . . About three weeks after he enlisted he was a second class petty officer with a motor mechs rating, on a subchaser which he kept going for the rest of the war. I believe he was discharged some time between the armistice signing and the end of the year, 1918. There are no records when he opened his shop but knowing him he probably wasted no time getting back to work.[14]

My suspicion was thus confirmed: Miller could not have printed either the *Portrait of Joseph Pennell* or *New York Bouquet* [Griffith 2],[15] which were drawn in November 1917, and exhibited, together with *North River*, at Frederick Keppel and Company in December of that year. Neither could he have printed the transfer lithographs that Hassam drew in the spring or summer of 1918; there would not have been time to print them between his return from military service and the opening of a second Hassam exhibition at Frederick Keppel on 3 December 1918. Given this fact, it is reasonable to conclude that Miller printed only one of the forty-five lithographs listed by Griffith and to speculate that all of the prints Hassam made during the spring of 1918—whether transfers or drawings on stone—may have been printed at Oberly and Newell. Having established a working relationship with Herr Faust, it is unlikely that Hassam would have been motivated to take his transfers elsewhere. *Camouflage* [Griffith 8] was drawn on 16 April (Griffith misread the date as 18 April), and *Virginia* [Griffith 10] was drawn on 23 April, just before and just after Hassam drew *The Lithographer* on stone on 22 April. *Camouflage*, a transfer, drawn from a vantage point above the Hudson River ("arrested for this," Hassam noted on the print[16]), is closely related to *The French Cruiser*, a lithotint on stone, printed by Faust. Is it reasonable to believe that on nearly consecutive days Hassam should have shuttled back and forth from one printer to another? The evidence may be circumstantial, but I think it is sufficient to support the premise that Faust printed most, if not all, of Hassam's transfer lithographs.

The sequence in which Hassam's prints were made is a separate issue to be determined. In the preface to his catalogue, Griffith stated that he had arranged the lithographs "in their apparent order of execution, as indicated by the date on the print." Although Hassam dated many of his lithographs, often providing the day and month as well as the year, the dates are sometimes obscured by strokes of his brush or crayon and are easy to misinterpret.[17]

A special problem is presented by *The Broad Curtain*, a lithotint not mentioned by Hassam in his manuscript. Griffith read the date of this print (written unclearly below Hassam's signature) as "Aug. 1, 1918," at which time Hassam was in Gloucester. Alternatively, the date could be read as April 1918 (the vertical line that Griffith interpreted as the number one could instead be the *l* in April), a change that would permit the print to be seen as a further statement in the series begun with the two versions of *Mrs. Hassam Knitting* [Griffith 6 and 7]. It would then become the first of the four lithotints made by Hassam in April and May.

The last of Hassam's transfer lithographs, *Avenue of the Allies* [Griffith 43] and *Return of the Fleet* [Griffith 44], are dated 19 October and 26 December 1918. Griffith gives no reason for placing the remarkable lithotint *Storm King* [Griffith 45], which is dated 1918, at the end of his catalogue. Are we to believe that Hassam drew it on stone, at the workshop of a commercial lithographer such as Oberly and Newell, during the holiday period between 26 and 31 December? Is it not more likely that it was drawn, along with the other lithotints, earlier in the year?

Hassam made no lithographs after 1918. Understandably, he may have been disappointed that so few were sold at his December exhibition (or thereafter).[18] In 1919 Hassam purchased a home in East Hampton, Long Island, and spent the summers there. Perhaps because of his increasingly lengthy absences from the city, perhaps because he had never established an extended collaborative relationship with a printer who special-

ized in work for artists—a relationship such as the one that developed between George Bellows and Bolton Brown—Hassam was unable to overcome a simplistic misperception of lithography's potential: the notion (as Hassam wrote) that "one machine will print the lithograph like another machine. . . . You may see all of these processes [of transferring and printing] at any lithographer's and know that they are frankly mechanical and learn all that there is to know about them in ten minutes."[19]

Despite the brilliance and audacity of some prints, Hassam's experience of lithography was a limited one: limited by the disruptions of the war; limited by the changing aesthetic climate, in which conservative and modernist styles uneasily coexisted; and limited by the fact that his work in the medium came both a bit too late, in terms of his own artistic development, and a moment too soon, in terms of the collaborative resources then available. We can only speculate as to the lithographs Hassam might have made if, continuing to work in 1919 and beyond, he had had the opportunity to work closely with Miller or with Brown—an artist-printer whose style would have been congenial to his own. In collaboration with either of these printers, Hassam would have had an opportunity to discover and explore a world of lithography of which he had only intimations. On the evidence of his work, the history of the American lithography would have been much the richer.

Notes

1. Clinton Adams, *American Lithographers, 1900–1960: The Artists and Their Printers* (Albuquerque: University of New Mexico Press, 1983).
2. Elisabeth Cary, "Childe Hassam and his Prints: A Compendium of Comment," *Prints* 6 (October 1935): 5.
3. For information about the Painter-Gravers of

America, we have long relied upon the account given in Ralph Flint, *Albert Sterner: His Life and Work* (New York: Payson & Clarke, 1927), 28. Flint erroneously gives the date of the organizational meeting as 9 January 1915, which Richard Field corrects in *American Prints 1900–1950* (New Haven: Yale University Art Gallery, 1983), 21–22. Field reports that a "copy of the *First Annual Year Book of the Painter-Gravers of America* at Harvard clearly establishes that the founding date was 9 January 1917 (and not 1915)." This correction serves to explain Hassam's presence as a charter member (and initial chairman) of the organization.

4. For more about Miller's early career, see Adams, *American Lithographers*, 24–28.

5. Fuller Griffith, *The Lithographs of Childe Hassam: A Catalog* (Washington, D.C.: Smithsonian Institution, Bulletin 232, 1962; reprint, New York: Martin Gordon, 1980).

6. *George Miller and American Lithography*, exhibition catalogue, text by Janet A. Flint (Washington, D.C.: National Collection of Fine Arts, Smithsonian Institution, 1976).

Miller's list is included in an undated advertising flyer, "Lithographic Printing for Artists," a copy of which is in the print room clipping files at the New York Public Library. I express my gratitude to the library and to Roberta Waddell, curator of prints, for invaluable assistance.

The sale was held at the Plaza Book Auction Corporation, New York, 23 March 1934. The print sold, though listed as *The Fleet on the Hudson*, must have been *North River*.

7. The firm of Oberly and Newell maintained its lithographic pressroom at 389 Lafayette Street. Herbert C. Newell was director of the firm.

8. Childe Hassam, in an unpublished, hand-written, autobiographical manuscript in the collection of the American Academy of Arts and Letters; hereinafter cited as Hassam manuscript. (A portion of this journal has been microfilmed by the Archives of American Art, Smithsonian Institution, reel NAA-1.) Herr Faust may have been George W. Faust, the only person of that name listed as a printer in the *New York City Directory* for 1918.

9. I gratefully acknowledge the support given to my research by the Cedar Rapids Museum of Art.

10. Elisabeth Cary, "Childe Hassam," 5.

11. For a discussion of the conservative attitudes that dominated Hassam's thinking after 1913, the year in which he participated in the Armory Show, see Donelson F. Hoopes, *Childe Hassam* (New York: Watson-Guptill, 1979), 16–20.

For a discussion of the "nude in nature" as a central theme in Fauvist and Expressionist painting, see Robert Goldwater, *Primitivism in Modern Art* (New York: 1938; rev. ed., New York: Vintage Books, 1967), 89–95, 109–12.

12. I am indebted to David Acton for many valuable suggestions and, specifically, for information about this design. See also Melvin and Betty Jahss, *Inro and Other Miniature Forms of Japanese Lacquer Art* (Rutland, Vt.: Charles E. Tuttle, 1971), 315. I am unable to determine the source of the watermarked paper; no print curator with whom I have corresponded is aware of its use in prints other than Hassam's.

13. As examples, the impressions of *Nude* in the New York Public Library and the Worcester Art Museum are printed on the back of engravings, on sheets of old laid paper.

14. Burr Miller to Adams, 21 March 1988.

15. *New York Bouquet* is closely related to a painting of the same title, dated 1917, oil on canvas. Illustrated, catalogue no. 102, in *Childe Hassam 1859–1935* (Tucson: University of Arizona Museum of Art, 1972).

16. "Childe Hassam, the artist, was arrested in Riverside Park yesterday for sketching a camouflaged American transport anchored in the Hudson. One look was enough for a passing gentleman and Mr. Hassam was delivered into the hands of the Federal Authorities. He had no difficulty in proving that he was innocent of knowingly violating the war regulations and was promptly released. Mr. Hassam then congratulated the policeman, saying that if every one was so alert there would not be as many dangerous enemy aliens travelling about the country" ("Childe Hassam Arrested," *New York Times*, 17 April 1918). The arrest did not deter Hassam from publishing the lithograph.

17. The dates on Hassam's transfer lithographs are, presumably, the dates of the drawings. Those made in Gloucester during the summer of 1918 were most likely transferred and printed after the artist's return to the city in the fall.

18. Most of the lithographs remained unsold at the time of Hassam's death in 1935 and were later distributed among American museums as gifts of Mrs. Hassam.

19. Hassam manuscript.

6 | WANDA GÁG'S
A Reconsideration of the Prints
FREE SPIRIT

RICHARD COX AND
JULIE L'ENFANT

THE STORY OF HOW WANDA GÁG went from Minnesota to New York in 1918 and attained fame as a children's book illustrator is now familiar. Although her achievements as a gallery printmaker are less well known, the recently published catalogue raisonné of the prints should introduce them to a wider public.[1] Nearly twenty years ago, coauthor Richard Cox was the first to discuss the place of Gág's prints in American art and culture.[2] His premise then was that Gág's graphic art was shaped by humanitarian-socialist beliefs stemming from her close friendship with another Minnesota artist, Adolf Dehn, and their involvement with the Greenwich village crowd of Floyd Dell, Max Eastman, and William Gropper. This viewpoint still has merit but should be modified to take into account new views on women artists and fresh information about Gág revealed in the diary she kept between 1920 and 1944, inaccessible to scholars until 1987.[3] Deserving particular attention are Gág's urge

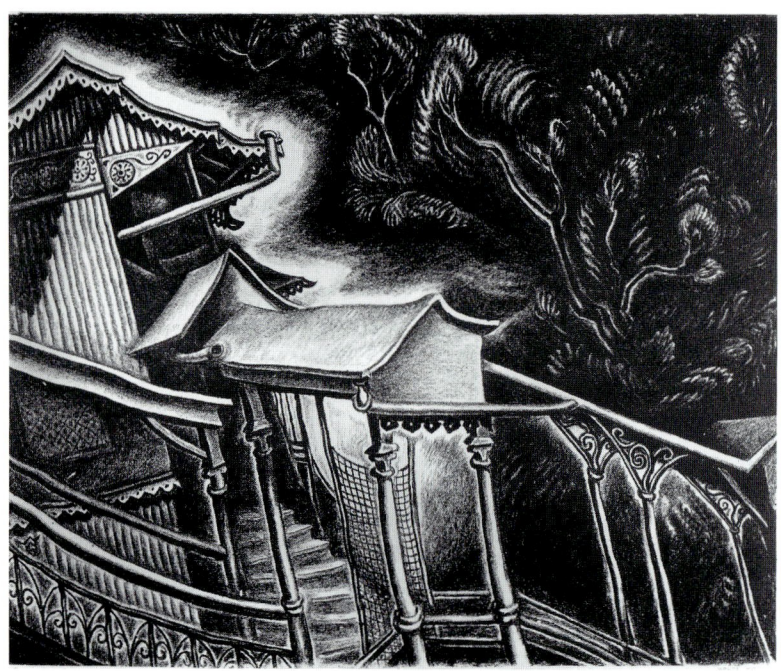

6.1 WANDA GÁG. *Elevated Station*, 1926. Transfer lithograph, 34 x 40.4 cm (image). Collection, Minneapolis Institute of Arts, gift of Dr. and Mrs. John E. Larkin, Jr. (P.87.13.6).

for sexual liberation and her strongly romanticist creed of nature worship.

Wanda Gág was on the fringe of the New York art world until her first one-artist exhibition of lithographs at the Weyhe Gallery in November 1926—a wildly successful debut. Carl Zigrosser brought Gág into the Weyhe inner circle; he also squired her around Manhattan, broadening her cultural outlook and introducing her to such people as Henry McBride, Alfred Stieglitz, and Georgia O'Keeffe. And, of course, to George C. Miller, who printed most of her lithographs.[4] Further exhibitions at the Weyhe Gallery in 1928 and 1930 heightened her reputation in New York, although she would achieve national fame only with *Millions of Cats* (1928) and later books for children.

The extravagant attitude at the heart of Gág's work is already apparent in prints of the 1920s that deal with the city. *Elevated Station*, a sly commentary on the urban jungle, transforms the conventional wooden station at Columbus Avenue and 81st Street into

a luminous, pulsating creature as alive as the swirling trees (figure 6.1). Gág's el station does not have the rambunctious human activity of an image by John Sloan or the futuristic allure of Louis Lozowick. It is closer to the puckish humor of her comrade Adolf Dehn, as seen in the rococo flourishes and blowsy satire of his 1922 Vienna lithographs.[5] Gág also spoofed the gospel of industrial progress in *Skyscraper* (1928) and *Stone Crusher* (1929). Her skepticism came partly from midwestern prejudice, but even more from seven long years in commercialistic New York. She is in accord with many another artist frustrated and disillusioned by modern life.[6]

This alienation helped steer Gág toward nature themes. After 1925 she lived in rented farmhouses away from the city in a mix of discomfort and bliss. She took to the simple life, walking barefoot in the woods and swimming naked in nearby lakes. She loved to set forth into the Kittatanny Mountains to "do battle with the hills."[7] Frank Walts gave her a copy of Adolf Just's *Return to Nature*, which, along with the writings of Thoreau, Van Gogh, and Franz Marc, helped shape her rustic philosophy.[8] A sprightly 1926 print, *Tumble Timbers* (named for her farmhouse in northwest New Jersey) expresses Gág's Rousseau-like creed (figure 6.2). Tumble Timbers had no heat or running water, but Gág delighted in its ramshackle appearance, going so far as to argue the landlord out of repairing its sagging porch. Comparison of the study drawing with the final work shows that Gág condensed the form of the house and simplified the textures of its materials. The ridges of the porch roof and fence boards are given exaggerated curves, and the plants in the garden embrace the house, as if to illustrate a unity of life and art that Gág had described in a letter to Dehn: "All about me there is a glorious fitting together of things,

60

Richard Cox and
Julie L'Enfant

round smooth faces with corresponding sockets; sharp painful angles with their complementary shapes; long vivid jags into crevices that hold them perfectly and calmly, so to restore the equanimity and rightness of things; and most of all perhaps, long tendrilly jutterings—out to receive and organize all the helpless fringes and frayed edges of our groping lives."[9]

Spring in the Garden (1927), *Gumbo Lane* (1927; figure 6.3), and *Sunset* (1929) also fashion nature into a stylized Eden. The swelling leafy forms and lurching fence posts, the throbbing ovals of trees and hillsides, and the intermingling of both natural and man-made forms show Gág's growing excitement about the country as well as her investigations into the sensuous art of Van Gogh, Marc, and various artists of Gallery 291, notably O'Keeffe, Charles Demuth, Arthur Dove, and Edward Weston. Clearly there is an erotic component to Gág's nature worship. As far back as 1915 her diary had been dominated by musings about her amours—her puppy love for Edgar Hermann in her Minneapolis art school days, her fitful romance with Dehn in New York, then her fully aroused sexual passion for Earle Humphreys after Dehn left for Europe in 1922. Gág desired a vigorous sex life for various reasons, but principally to enrich her art. "It is not a matter of morality to me," she wrote in her diary, "it is a matter of health and art."[10] This rapturous union of drawing and sex is most evident in her garden and hillside prints. A description of daisies on a hilltop recalls D. H. Lawrence: "There is an exuberance and lavishness about the foliage that is intoxicating and the lascivious plenitude of their form fills me with primitivism. . . . I want to tear off all my clothes and lie among the grasses."[11] Trees were often the focus of her élan vital: in fact, one of her code names for sexual intercourse

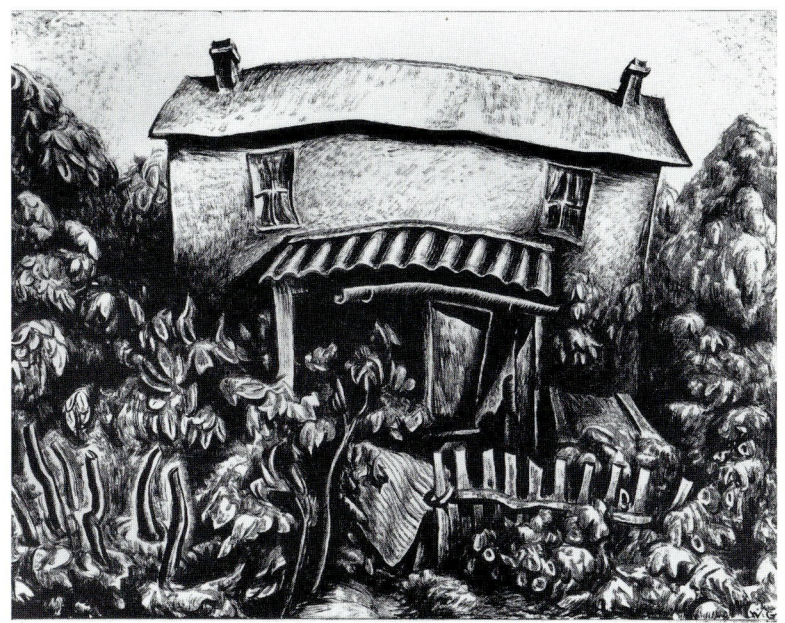

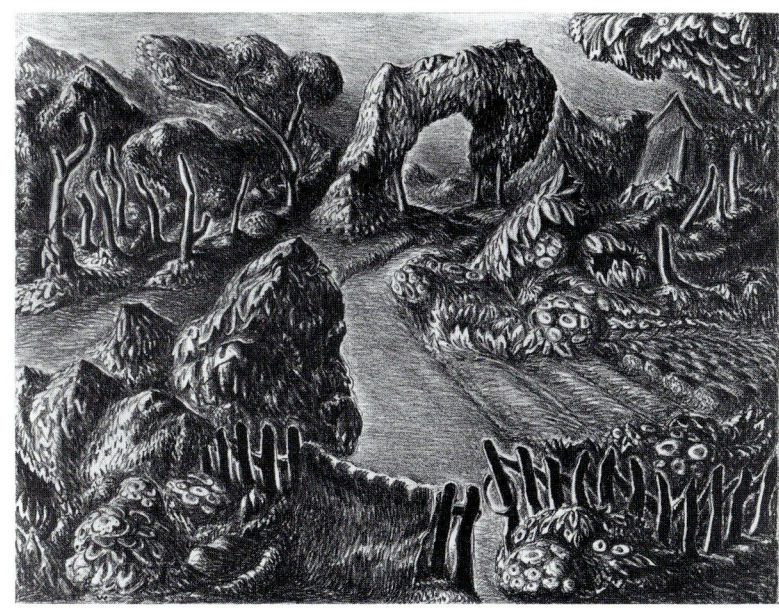

6.2 WANDA GÁG. *Tumble Timbers*, 1926. Wash lithograph, 22 x 28.2 cm (image). Collection, Minneapolis Institute of Arts, gift of Dr. and Mrs. John E. Larkin, Jr. (P.87.13.4).

6.3 WANDA GÁG. *Gumbo Lane*, 1927. Lithograph, 25.3 x 32.7 cm (image). Collection, Minneapolis Institute of Arts, gift of Dr. and Mrs. John E. Larkin, Jr. (P.87.13.7).

was *treetop,* which she linked to artistic form and space. "Perspective has . . . an ecstatic effect upon me—I remember the time that I had a climax (in the midst of a treetop with Earle) while and because of thinking of the mathematical recession of planes."[12] Indian erotic art, where lotus blossoms atop the human head represent the ecstatic burst of orgasm, probably played a part in Gág's ideas.[13]

Wanda Gág did not merely theorize or fantasize: she lived out her notions of the free-spirited, hedonistic woman. She was fitted for a birth control device by an associate of Margaret Sanger in 1922, when this was still a shocking thing for a single woman to do. Three years later she had an abortion. She lived unmarried with Earle Humphreys through much of the 1920s and 1930s, meanwhile carrying on affairs with Zigrosser, Howard Cook, Hugh Darby, and perhaps others. She enjoyed the game of seduction, of being pursued and propositioned by well-known men. She admired O'Keeffe's persona as a self-sufficient woman and did not understand why O'Keeffe grew so indignant over erotic interpretations of her flower paintings. It was ever Gág's aim to lift her art and life to ecstatic heights. Sometimes her love life became nerve-racking. Once, to calm herself from the strain of her triangle with Humphreys and Zigrosser, she resolved to read John Ruskin.[14]

It is tempting to see Gág as just another voluptuary caught up in the flapper-age vogue for free love, but her life and art raise serious feminist issues. She defied the stereotype that women artists were incapable of abstract thought and limited to an art of superficial impressions.[15] In Gág's work, layers of eroticism and romantic symbolism deepen the meaning. Gág also bucked the notion that female artists could develop only the sensory side of art, especially color, as opposed to the rational side, marked by the skills in composition and drawing thought to come naturally to men.[16] Like Mary Cassatt, whose ability in drypoint had startled Degas, Gág's strong suit was drawing, and she worked almost exclusively in black and white. Her increasingly streamlined compositions reveal an analytical concentration equal to that of any American printmaker of her generation.

The diary reveals Gág's struggles to impose order on her art. Often she turned to Cézanne's drawings to "tame the swirling planes" and "whip into submission [her] drawing moods." Pages of the diary are filled with diagrams and schematic plans: form was a particular preoccupation and, with an increasing desire for more volume and depth in the prints, space as well. "There is, to me, no such thing as an empty place in the universe —and if Nature abhors a vacuum, so do I— and I am just as eager as nature to fill a vacuum with something . . . at least with a tiny rhythm of its own, that is a rhythm created by its surrounding forms."[17]

The subdued mood and tightened structure of lithographs between 1929 and 1934 show Gág's deep affection for preindustrial objects. These still lifes and interior scenes, such as *Evening* (1928), *Lamplight* (1929; figure 6.4), and *Backyard Corner* (1930), give rapt attention to the old lamps, spinning wheels, Franklin stoves, and plows that express nostalgia for the rural values of her childhood in the Bohemian-Hungarian community of New Ulm, Minnesota. *Lamplight* is a strong, simplified image reflecting life at Tumble Timbers, which had no electricity. It expresses a homely beauty and intimacy by means of interlocking shapes and forms. Indeed, the knobby forms and poignant light remind us of Van Gogh, another artist who identified with peasant ways.[18] These Gág prints reveal the meditative side of the artist,

Richard Cox and
Julie L'Enfant

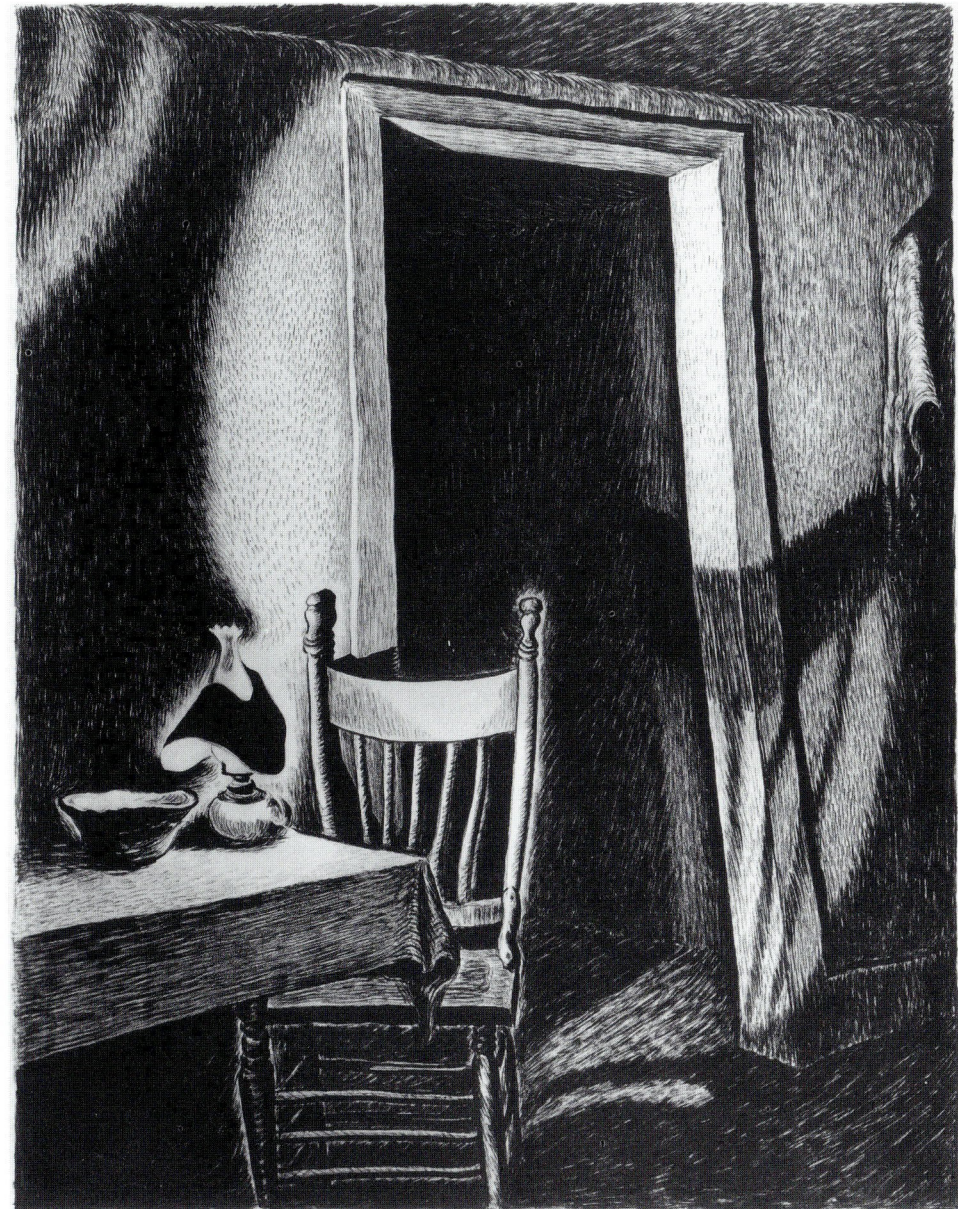

who craved privacy that she might ponder the deeper meanings of ordinary objects—lamps or washbowls, quilts or stoves—as if they were pieces of fine crystal. The quiet, intimate spirit is akin to that of Edward Hopper or Yasuo Kuniyoshi.

Until her death in 1946 Gág would feel ill at ease with urban America, with its hurried pace, unsightly advertising, and business-first mentality, all sharply satirized in her 1936 lithograph *Progress* (figure 6.5). She preferred unspoiled nature and a society built on the idealistic socialist ideas that had been current in Greenwich Village during her early New York years.[19] As her diary makes clear, however, Wanda Gág developed these dreams of a just and free-spirited life into a deeper romanticist creed, where a Dionysian model of

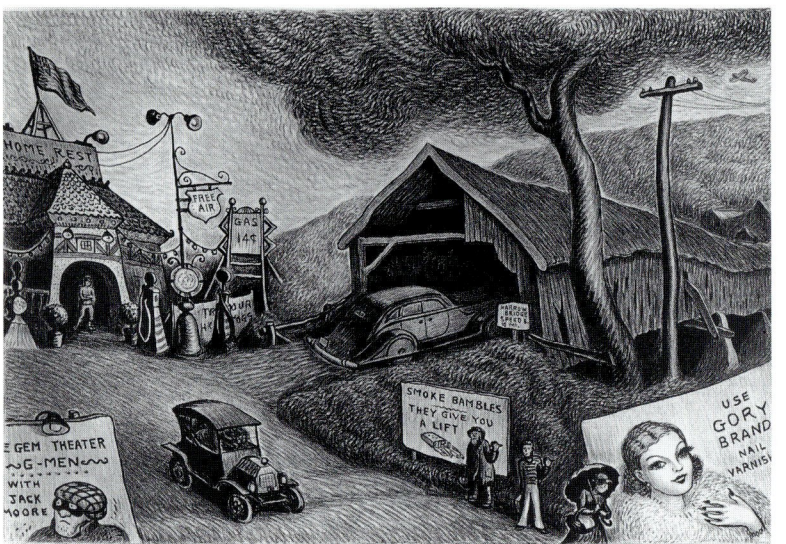

6.5 WANDA GÁG.
Progress, 1936. Lithograph,
20.8 x 30 cm (image).
Collection, Minneapolis
Institute of Arts, gift of
the estate of Wanda Gág
(P.12,464).

creativity connected her vigorous sex drive
to the making of art.

NOTES

1. Audur H. Winnan, *Wanda Gág: A Catalogue Raisonné of the Prints* (Washington, D.C.: Smithsonian Institution Press, 1993).
2. Richard Cox, "Wanda Gág: The Bite of the Picture Book," *Minnesota History* (fall 1975): 239–53.
3. These diaries were deposited in the Wanda Gág Collection, Department of Special Collections, Van Pelt Library, University of Pennsylvania. Diaries and letters in this collection are hereafter cited as VPL.
4. In 1926 Gág wrote that she was in "awe of Zigrosser's culture and good judgement" and commented on his "glamorous and gentlemanly" personality (Diary, VPL, 19 January 1926). On Miller's printing of Gág's lithographs, Gág's work with other printers, and technical matters concerning the linocuts and wood-engravings, see Winnan, 86–88.
5. See Clinton Adams, "Adolf Dehn: The Lithographs," in *The Prints of Adolf Dehn: A Catalogue Raisonné*, Jocelyn Pang Lumsdaine and Thomas O'Sullivan, comps. (St. Paul: Minnesota Historical Society Press, 1987), 28–29.
6. On Gág's scorn of business-dominated urban

America, see Diary, VPL, 27 February and 5 July 1924. On artists' disillusionment with modern life, see Nigel Blake and Francis Frascina, "Modern Practices of Art and Modernity," in *Modernity and Modernism: French Painting in the Nineteenth Century* (New Haven: Yale University Press, 1993), 129–30.
7. Diary, VPL, 9 January 1928.
8. Diary, VPL, 27 February 1924. For references to Van Gogh see 15 June 1929 and 3 March 1930. For Thoreau, see 27 February 1924.
9. Gág to Dehn, Dehn papers, Archives of American Art, Smithsonian Institution, December 1921.
10. Diary, VPL, 2 April 1920.
11. Diary, VPL, 21 June 1922. Gág related this "liberation" to her disdain for the business world. Feeling that her whole sense of the body had been perverted by commercial art, she renounced the human figure and immersed herself in nature, studying rocks, hills, and clouds in an effort to arrive at their essences (Diary, VPL, 6 July 1923).
12. Diary, VPL, June 1935.
13. Lucile Blanch, Gág's close friend in New York from 1918 to 1922, remembered that Gág and Dehn shared books on Indian erotic art and egged each other on to include more erotica in their work. Richard Cox interview with Lucile Blanch, Woodstock, New York, 30 May 1975. See also Diary, VPL, 2 May 1921.
14. On O'Keeffe, see Diary, VPL, 18 January, 8 February, and 25 August 1928, and 14 February 1931. On reading Ruskin, see Diary, VPL, 19 June 1926.
15. See Tamar Garb, "Gender and Representation," in *Modernity and Modernism*, 280–89.
16. Ibid., esp. 284–85.
17. Diary, VPL, May 1926, 9 January 1928, and 29 October 1929.
18. See Ross Neher, "Van Gogh's Problem with Tradition," *Arts* 65 (January 1987): 43–48.
19. See William O'Neill, *Echoes of Revolt: The Masses, 1911–1917* (Chicago: Quadrangle Books, 1966), esp. 17–33, for a discussion of Greenwich Village radicalism. See also Floyd Dell, *Love in Greenwich Village* (New York: George H. Doran, 1926), especially "The Kitten and the Masterpiece," 47–73 and "The Ex-Villager's Confession," 239–51.

7 | PAINTER,

A Further Investigation of

MANNIKIN,

the Prints of Arshile Gorky

AND MIRROR

ROBERT P. CONWAY

IN 1965 JO MILLER, ASSISTANT curator of prints at the Brooklyn Museum, published the first organized account of the prints of Arshile Gorky.[1] During the past thirty years, her article has served as our standard point of reference whenever Gorky's rare and enigmatic images have appeared on the market or in exhibitions. By returning to the original checklists of the *American Printmakers, Fifth Annual Exhibition at the Downtown Gallery*, where Gorky's lithographs were first shown in 1931, Miller corrected several basic errors that had accumulated in the literature. She established that there were two major images, *Mannikin* and *Painter and Model*, instead of one, as had been reported the previous year in *ArtNews*.[2] She gave them their correct titles, dates, and measurements, and dispelled the notion that they existed in proofs only.[3] She identified four known impressions of *Mannikin* and established at least the theoretical existence of an edition by citing the numbering, 23/25, on the impression purchased from the Downtown Gallery at the time of the original exhibition by Abby Aldrich Rockefeller and later given to the Museum of Modern Art. Miller made accurate connections between the images and their sources both in Gorky's paintings and in those of Pablo Picasso, one of Gorky's primary influences. Finally, she established the existence of a third lithograph, a *Self-Portrait,* as well as a serigraph and a woodblock Christmas card.[4]

Miller modestly concluded her article with the hope that "this first endeavor to record the prints of Gorky will lead to discovery of other unknown prints, and that a full checklist of the artist's graphic work will eventually be forthcoming." Since 1964, however, no new images have been discovered, and it seems likely, though not certain, that her list will stand as the complete record of the artist's printmaking efforts. Even so, a few years ago a basic mistake in Miller's brief list became apparent by chance, an error that had been literally before her—and our—eyes for decades. The detection of this error and an explanation of its nature and significance are the subject of this article.[5]

In its sale *American, Modern and Contemporary Prints* (10 May 1988, lot 25), Christie's listed and illustrated an impression of *Mannikin.* Both the illustration and the work itself were printed in reverse of the photograph published by Miller. I initially explained the seeming contradiction to myself by assuming that her photograph had been mistakenly "flopped" during the printing of the Brooklyn article.[6] At the time, nobody, apparently, approached this question with the unlikely assumption that *both* photographs were correct; more to the point, none of us then involved in this area of the print market compared the Christie's impression with the impression illustrated by Miller. As she noted, Gorky gave this impression in the mid-1930s to Hans Burkhardt, a

pupil and colleague who, until his death in 1994, was very actively painting and making prints in Los Angeles.[7]

Two years later, in their sale *Historical and American Prints* (18 January 1990, lot 148), Christie's offered an impression of *Painter and Model.* Again, both the catalogue illustration and the print itself were in reverse of the photograph published by Miller, as well as in reverse of an impression then in the inventory of the Associated American Artists (AAA) gallery in New York.[8] This time the evidence was too compelling to overlook: two impressions in the same city at the same time were mirror images of each other. After the auction, both impressions were examined side by side at the gallery, and it was clear to those who examined them that one was not a redrawn variant of the other. They appeared to be exact replicas, line for line and dot for dot, but one was printed in reverse of the other. At this time, however, no conclusions were drawn as to how or why they were made.

The fourth and final piece of this puzzle fell into place in 1992, when I saw the Burkhardt impression of *Mannikin,* illustrated over the years by Rosenberg, *ArtNews,* and Miller.[9] Miller, in fact, had not flopped her photograph. Both the Burkhardt impression and Miller's photograph were the reverse of the 1988 Christie's impression, just as the AAA impression and Miller's photograph of *Painter and Model* were the reverse of the 1990 Christie's impression. It was clear, finally, that both of Gorky's lithographs existed as mirror opposites.

In consultation with three experts in the field, Clinton Adams, director emeritus of Tamarind Institute; Melvin Lader, professor of art at George Washington University; and David Kiehl, curator of prints at the Whitney Museum of American Art, I organized an informal conference at the Whitney Museum

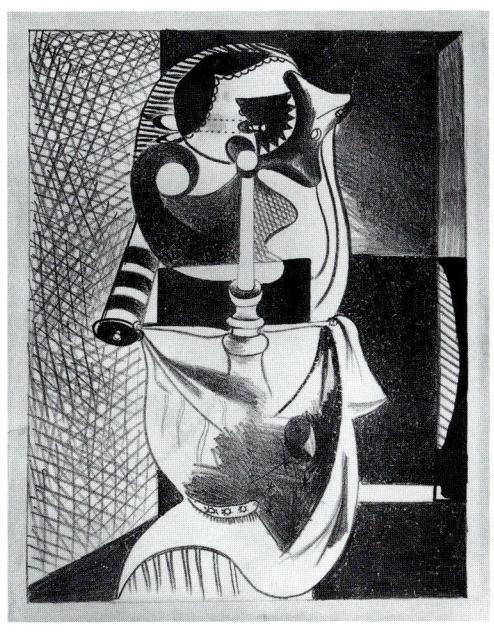

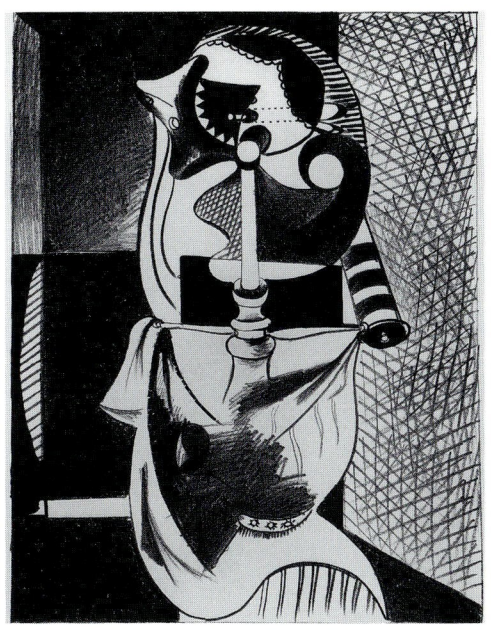

7.1 ARSHILE GORKY. *Mannikin,* (1931). Lithograph, 37.6 x 28.9 cm. Collection, Hans and Thordis Burkhardt, gift of the artist.

7.2 ARSHILE GORKY. *Mannikin,* (1931). Lithograph, 37.4 x 28.9 cm. Collection, Reba and Dave Williams.

in November 1993, which brought together, possibly for the first time since they were printed in 1931, an impression of each image in each orientation.[10] By the time of this meeting, a census of existing impressions had been prepared and we were able to replace the confusing terminology of "reversed" impressions (Which was the reverse of which?) and the prejudicial label "original" orientation (No visual or written evidence yet proved conclusively that one orientation preceded the other) with the more neutral and more accurate terms, "majority" and "minority." A majority impression was one that belonged to the larger group of impressions, all printed in the same orientation; a minority impression was printed in the opposite orientation. So far, we know of ten impressions of *Mannikin* in the majority group; the Burkhardt impression, and possibly one other, form the minority. Twelve impressions of *Painter and Model* comprise the majority, while the minority consists of the Christie's impression, now in the collection of Dave and Reba Williams, and possibly one other.[11]

Present at the meeting were David Kiehl, with the Whitney's majority impression of *Mannikin;* myself, with the Burkhardt minority impression of *Mannikin* (figure 7.1); Dave Williams, with another majority impression of *Mannikin* (the 1988 Christie's impression), as well as the 1990 Christie's minority impression of *Painter and Model* (figures 7.2 and 7.3); and Linda Kramer and Karen Zieve, then curator and assistant curator of the Department of Prints and Drawings at the Brooklyn Museum, with the majority impression of *Painter and Model* (figure 7.4) that originally stimulated Miller to write her article. Because of unfortunate scheduling conflicts, neither Clinton Adams nor Mel Lader were able to attend, but by an equally fortunate scheduling coincidence, our small company was increased by Antony Griffiths, head keeper of the Department of Prints and Drawings at the British Museum.[12]

First, the five sheets were matched with their opposites, and each was examined closely to determine that they were in fact mirror opposites sharing the most minute

67

Painter, Mannikin,
and Mirror

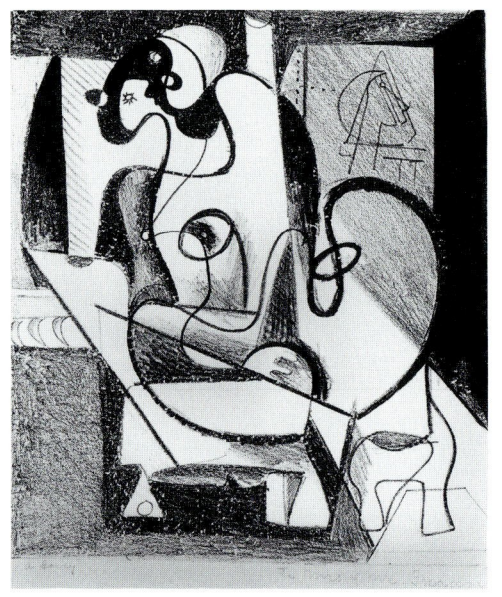
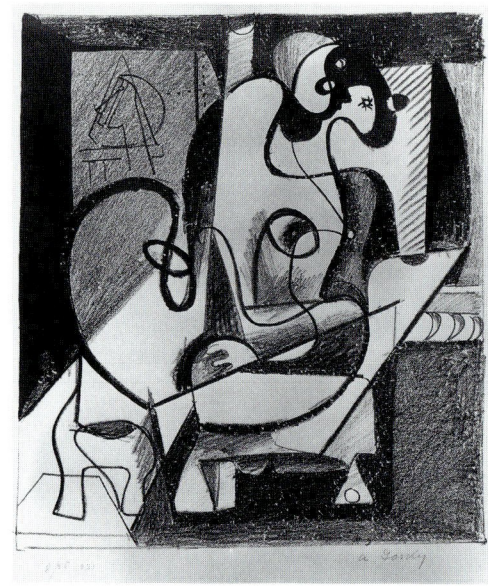

nuances of line. Then, all were measured, papers examined, and the quality of impressions compared. In all cases, the measurements of both image and sheet for each pair were the same, given an allowance of a millimeter or two for the stretching of the paper when printed. In both cases, the minority impressions of each image were printed on a slightly coarse, cream proofing paper, while the majority impressions were printed on a finer edition paper with either a *France* or *Rives* watermark. Most significantly, in both cases the minority impressions of each image differed slightly but noticeably in quality of printing from those in the majority. In all impressions, the lines and more lightly drawn areas of the two images were very closely comparable. In the darkest areas of both, the majority impressions were printed with a uniform black surface, while in the minority impressions these areas were somewhat mottled and without the solid surface (figures 7.5 and 7.6).

There are generally four possible ways in which reversed impressions of lithographs might be made: (1) by redrawing the image on a second matrix; (2) by pulling a counter-proof from an impression freshly printed from the matrix; (3) by printing some impressions directly and others on an offset press, with or without transfer of the image from a first to a second matrix; or (4) by reproducing and reversing the image photographically. Our observations clearly eliminated the first and fourth methods. Neither version of either image was the product of redrawing, because this sort of copying produces minute variation in the lines, particularly in the less prominent areas of the composition. To the limits of our perception, the impressions we saw appeared to be exact replicas of their opposites. Photographic reproduction produces exact replicas in the sense that all the marks of the original appear in the reproduction, but the visual quality of these marks differs because they have been applied to their matrices via different processes. Again, to the best of our observation, all the impressions we examined appear to have been printed from marks drawn directly onto a lithographic matrix.

The remaining possibilities, counterproofing and offset lithography, are more likely explanations. A counterproof is made by placing a blank sheet of paper against a newly printed impression and running them together through the press. It is often called a "ghost" because it receives only a portion of the ink that has been applied to the matrix for the printing of the first impression and is therefore more lightly inked than the impression from which it has been pulled. The relatively pale appearance of a counterproof can be strengthened by over-inking the matrix, especially the darker areas of the composition, before pulling the initial impression, but it is extremely difficult to print a counterproof whose values match those of its source as closely as do the pairs of Gorky lithographs.[13] The mottled printing of the dark areas of the minority impressions of both images suggests counterproofing, but their overall quality would be extremely difficult to achieve in a counterproof.

Offset lithography, then, seems to be the method used by Gorky and his printer. Use of the offset process avoids the reversal of the image that occurs in direct printing. Impressions printed by offset thus have an orientation opposite from those printed directly from a stone or plate.[14] In the case of the Gorky lithographs, questions remain, however, as to which version came first, and why Gorky and his printer should have gone to the trouble and expense of producing both prints both ways.

Two sequences are possible. In the first hypothetical sequence, a few minority impressions were printed as proofs from the original matrix. Not being satisfied with them, either because of their quality or because of the reversal of the image from his original drawing on the stone or plate (we cannot be certain which was used), either Gorky asked or the printer suggested that they switch to offset.[15] The majority of the impressions were then printed by offset, and they comprise the editions as we know them

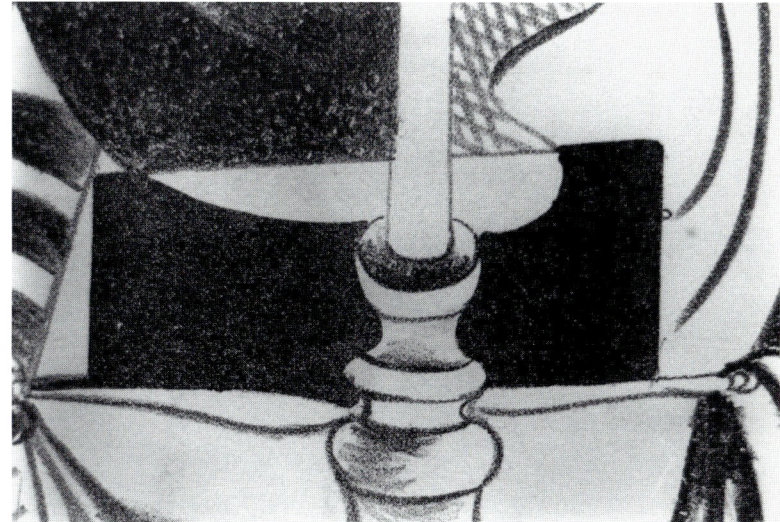

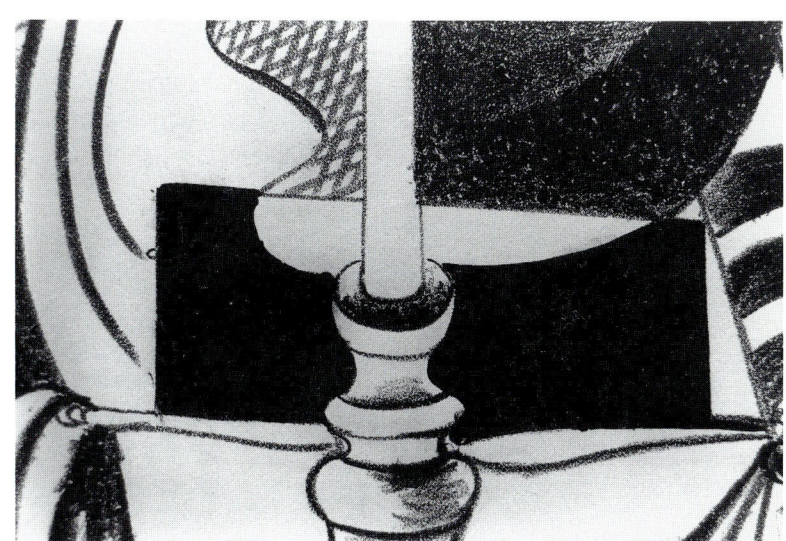

7.5 Detail: Minority (Burkhardt) impression of *Mannikin.*

7.6 Detail: Majority (Collier) impression of *Mannikin.*

today. In the second sequence, the impressions of the majority group were pulled from the original matrix; then Gorky and his printer briefly diverged into offset lithography to produce a few proofs in the opposite orientation.[16] Which is the more likely?

Offset lithographs may be printed from an initial, hand-drawn plate, which, in some instances, may also be proofed by hand;[17] alternatively, an offset plate may be made by transferring an image first drawn on another plate or on stone. When transfer is employed, the first issue to address is the relative quality of impressions pulled from an original matrix, when compared with those printed from a second offset plate. Burr Miller, the son of and successor to George Miller, knows from his experience in their shop that his father was able to transfer an image to an offset plate so carefully that not one dot would be lost. He allowed, however, that in the first pass through the press a sheet printed by offset might not adequately carry the rich, glossy black areas and would come out mottled. It was his practice to run impressions through the press twice to achieve the rich dark areas, but this method invites problems with registration and has to be done very carefully.[18]

Miller's recollection seems to be consistent with our observation in the fall of 1993 of differences between the majority and minority impressions, and points toward the second sequence described above: that is, that the minority impressions, with mottled areas of printing, were pulled experimentally from an offset press. However, in the year following the Whitney meeting, I was able to examine six other majority impressions of both images, and found that the variation among them in the printing of the dark areas is almost as great as the differences first noticed between pairs of minority and majority impressions brought to the Whitney. A few majority impressions have uniformly glossy dark areas; in others, these areas are solid but flat, rather than glossy. In still others, the flat inking gives way to mottled areas. Out of the total of twenty-six recorded impressions for both images, only twenty have been located. Within this group of twenty, the quality of the impressions follows a normal bell-curve

distribution: a few outstanding impressions, a larger number of "normal" impressions, and a few lesser impressions.

What are we to make of this evidence? If we momentarily ignore the reversal of the images and consider only the quality of their printing and the character of the paper on which they are printed, the distinctions between minority and majority impressions blur into a continuum ranging from mottled to shiny black. On this range, the most noticeable mottling of the minority "proofs" may be as much the result of the absorption of ink into the porous paper as of the methods by which they were printed. We must admit that the quality of impression is not as reliable a basis as we might have hoped for connecting the mottled impressions to use of offset printing

Our other evidence is similarly ambiguous. The printing of the two known minority impressions on proofing paper supports their status as experimental proofs, but gives us no indication of whether they were printed directly or by offset. Hans Burkhardt's repeated description of his minority impression of *Mannikin* as a proof done before any edition was printed supports our first sequence, in which the minority impressions were printed from the original matrix and the majority of the edition was reversed by offset.[19] That Gorky signed the minority impression of *Painter and Model* and dedicated it to the then director of the Grand Central School of Art, but neither signed nor dedicated the minority impression of *Mannikin* that he gave to his colleague Burkhardt supports neither case, and suggests that the painter didn't differentiate as we do the status of proofs and editions, and that the orientation of the image, in the end, didn't make much difference to him.

Looking further for material that would

corroborate one or the other of our hypotheses, we find intriguing evidence on both sides. There are at least three extant drawings of compositions very close to *Painter and Model*, all apparently from the same sketchbook and all in private collections. Two show the subject in the orientation of the majority group of prints and one in the orientation of the minority impression.[20] Again, it seems that the direction of the composition may not have been a fixed element in the artist's relentless experimentation and development of his work.[21] Gorky's closely related painting, *Abstraction with Palette* (ca. 1930), now in the Philadelphia Museum of Art, is in the same orientation as the majority impressions of *Painter and Model*. Did Gorky want his edition to read in the same direction as the painting? If so, he could have anticipated the automatic reversal between matrix and impression and deliberately drawn the image on the stone in reverse to the painting—which we know he did in one of the sketchbook drawings mentioned above. It is possible, however, that as a neophyte not anticipating the initial reversal inherent in printmaking, he could have drawn on the stone or plate in the same direction as the painting, could have been surprised by impressions coming off the press in reverse, and thus chose to utilize offset in order to achieve a second reversal, back to the direction of the painting.[22]

This scenario, our first hypothesis, gains support from another bit of external evidence. A 1992–93 exhibition of works by Stuart Davis at AAA included a "reverse" impression of *Sixth Avenue El*, taken from the estate of the artist, printed the same year as Gorky's lithographs, and annotated, "Printer's Proof."[23] Davis was Gorky's close friend and was something of a mentor to the younger artist.[24] It is likely that Davis secured Gorky's acceptance into the show at the Downtown Gallery, and he may also have introduced him to George Miller, who printed *Sixth Avenue El* and possibly other editions for Davis.[25] What was Davis doing with a "reversed" proof? Its annotation as a printer's proof, like Burkhardt's recollection of Gorky calling his impression of *Mannikin* a "proof," suggests that it precedes the printing of the edition in the opposite orientation: the one we, until now, have assumed was the only one.[26] Did Gorky follow his lead and, out of a need to correct the orientation of his images, switch to offset before printing the editions? Or did both he and Davis print the odd offset impressions out of curiosity?[27]

The sum of the external evidence does not support conclusively either sequence. Nevertheless, we can assume with some confidence that the reversals were made by means of offset lithography. Both a hand press and an offset press can produce mottled dark tones. The question is which printing method is more likely to have produced the darker impressions that comprise the majority group of both subjects. Our most compelling visual evidence, the mottled areas of the minority impressions, suggests somewhat inconclusively that they are the offset prints and supports the second of the two hypotheses: that Gorky was in the habit of working a composition both ways and had one or more proofs printed experimentally in reverse to his edition. The logic of the workshop, however, suggests the opposite: that an image is transferred to offset in order to avoid its reversal when printed, to control the quality of the printing, and to produce multiple impressions quickly.

A definitive conclusion requires further evidence, and it seems appropriate for me to end my reinvestigation of Gorky's lithographs as Jo Miller did hers, with the hope that this effort to unravel an admittedly small bit of art history will lead to the discovery of information that will shed more light on this vital period in the development of lithography in America. In the larger context of Gorky's art, it may not really matter which scenario is the correct one, as either script for Gorky's brief encounter with lithography fits nicely his preoccupation with drawing in the first years of the decade, a period of intense development during which the facility and rapidity of that medium allowed him to experiment and change easily. As Diane Waldman noted in her essay for the Guggenheim Museum's 1981 retrospective of Gorky's work, his few paintings of the early thirties look back to his evolution from sources in the work of Cézanne and Picasso, while "the lithographs and drawings prefigure a new direction."[28] This new direction led Gorky to the unique synthesis of Cubism and Surrealism that was his singular contribution to the evolution of modern art, an early step leading from the assimilation of the European avant-garde toward a truly original, new style of painting in America.[29]

Notes

1. Jo Miller, "The Prints of Arshile Gorky," *Brooklyn Museum Annual* 6 (1964–65): 57–61.
2. *ArtNews* 62:2 (April 1963): 27, with an illustration of Hans Burkhardt's impression of *Mannikin,* labeled "Arshile Gorky's only lithograph."
3. Harold Rosenberg, *Arshile Gorky: The Man, the Time, the Idea* (New York: Grove Press, 1962), 49, first illustrated the Burkhardt impression of *Mannikin* with the title *Birth of a Nation,* and with an incorrect date (1936) and measurements (16 x 12 in.). For correct date and measurements of Gorky's lithographs, see captions to illustrations. The impression of *Painter and Model* in the collection of the National Museum of American Art bears the alternate title *The Creation Chamber.*
4. As Miller notes, the *Self-Portrait* was also in the Downtown Gallery's exhibition. No extant im-

pressions are known. The serigraph was in the collection of the artist's friend and biographer Ethel K. Schwabacher, but its present location is unknown. It relates to a Gorky painting in the Whitney Museum, and as Sylvan Cole has suggested in conversation, may be one of a somewhat mysterious group of screenprints after paintings by artists of the period, including Charles Burchfield, Ralston Crawford, Stuart Davis, Yasuo Kuniyoshi, Reginald Marsh, and Guy Pene du Bois. An impression of the Christmas card is in the collection of Dave and Reba Williams, New York.

5. I have approached the correction of Miller's work with the respect due her and her institution. In the 1950s and 1960s, the department of prints and drawings at the Brooklyn Museum was virtually alone in its acquisition and exhibition of American printmakers of the thirties, forties, and fifties. Without Miller's efforts, and those of Una E. Johnson, then director of the department, we would have no foundation from which to make further investigation into the work of many of the artists active in these years.
6. The same assumption, though in reverse, was made at the time of the publication of Miller's article by Riva Castleman, then cataloguer and now director of the Department of Prints and Illustrated Books at the Museum of Modern Art. In a February 1955 letter to Miller, Castleman noted that the *ArtNews* illustration must have been reversed, since it read opposite to the impression in MoMA's collection. This illustration, however, was in the same orientation as both the photograph published by Miller and the actual impression owned by Burkhardt. My thanks to Linda Kramer for allowing me access to Miller's correspondence.
7. Such a comparison would have been easy to make, as Burkhardt and his dealer, Jack Rutberg, have always been more than cooperative in my inquiries about these lithographs.
8. This impression is now in the collection of the Worcester Art Museum. I am grateful to David Acton for his interest in this project. His enthusiastic and knowledgeable exploration into forgotten areas of American printmaking has been a consistent inspiration for my own study of this field.
9. This impression remains in the collection of Hans and Thordis Burkhardt.
10. Clinton Adams was most helpful in analyzing the information and testing possible explanations of this problem. As an artist, lithographer, and art

historian specializing in the history of lithography, he is an invaluable resource for any investigation in this field. Melvin P. Lader, author of *Arshile Gorky, 1904–1948* (New York: Abbeville, ca. 1985) and the forthcoming catalogue raisonné of Gorky's drawings, generously gave me his census of the existing lithographs. David Kiehl, who in the last decade has organized several of the most original and important exhibitions on neglected aspects of American printmaking, provided both a place to meet and expert advice on how to approach this problem.

11. See the appendix for a census of existing impressions.

12. Under the direction of Griffiths and his colleague Frances Carey, the British Museum has collected a remarkable group of modern American prints and drawings that surpasses many institutional collections in this country.

13. Harry Sternberg, who was active as a printmaker in New York in the 1930s, told Linda Kramer, his niece, that the practice of heavy inking and counterproofing was commonplace at the time.

14. Dave and Reba Williams are compiling an informal record of other reversed pairs from the early decades of the century, including not only lithographs by Gorky but also by James Brooks, Stuart Davis, José Clemente Orozco, and Arnold Rönnebeck. The existence of these prints suggests that offset presses may have been used more commonly than previously supposed for the printing of hand-drawn lithographs.

15. Offset might also have been used if an original drawing on stone were damaged. It is unlikely, however, that two stones used by Gorky would crack at the same time.

16. These two hypotheses were suggested, respectively, by Clinton Adams and Antony Griffiths.

17. Jean Charlot, working with the Los Angles printer Lynton Kistler, produced many lithographs in this way. See Clinton Adams, *American Lithographers 1900–1960: The Artists and Their Printers* (Albuquerque: University of New Mexico Press, 1983), 100–102.

18. I am grateful to Burr Miller for taking the time for several lengthy telephone conversations between November 1993 and August 1994. He, his father, and his sons represent the finest tradition in American lithography.

19. Burkhardt's wife, Thordis, told Miller this in a letter of February 1965. It was confirmed several times in conversations between Burkhardt and Jack Rutberg.

20. Thanks to Mel Lader for providing photocopies of these three drawings.

21. Harold Rosenberg vividly describes the artist's attitude: "In Gorky's work of this period meticulousness reaches the point of obsession. He carries to completion composition after composition on the same themes, always in search of the perfect approximation to the work of the master. His drawings in ink run, in the space of a year, into the hundreds, into the thousands" (Rosenberg, *Arshile Gorky*, 71).

22. At the end of her article, Miller speculated that Gorky was not interested in the technical aspects of lithography but that, because of his extreme poverty, printed his lithographs himself. In the light of the four different versions of his prints, it now seems more likely that he was interested in the technique, at least enough to exploit it for his own ends, but that he did not print them himself, as he could not be expected to master the skills needed for offset printing. See Adams, *American Lithographers*, 77n.

23. *Stuart Davis, Drawings, Prints and Paintings* (New York: Associated American Artists, 1992), number 39.

24. Lader, *Arshile Gorky*, 37.

25. Burr Miller recalls his father having worked with Davis and thinks Gorky may also have come to the shop. Clinton Adams has informed me of a list from George Miller's 1934 auction of shop inventory that includes a proof of Davis's *Sixth Avenue El*. On the other hand, Adams has raised the possibility that Miller may not have printed for Gorky, as he did not have an offset press in his shop in the early thirties and did not include Gorky's name on an extensive list of artists (published after 1940) with whom he had worked. Another likely printer would be J. E. Rosenthal, who printed for Downtown Gallery artist Max Weber and who used an offset press in the twenties and thirties. Adams has also noted in conversation several other circumstances that point to Rosenthal as a likely printer for Gorky: Arnold Rönnebeck, whose reversed images are mentioned in n. 14 above, was a friend of Pop Hart, who is known to have printed with Rosenthal. Orozco, cited in the same note, printed first with Miller in 1928, then "switched the next year to another, cheaper printer" in New York (see Adams, *Amer-*

ican Lithographers, 97–98). Might that have been Rosenthal? Finally, the varied quality of printing in Gorky's editions is contrary to what we see as the hallmark of Miller's work: his consistent high quality. Perhaps Orozco's move from one printer to another parallels Gorky's shift from direct to offset printing. If we could conclusively place Gorky in Rosenthal's workshop, working from the start on a zinc plate to be printed by offset, as was Rosenthal's standard procedure, we would have the following simple and likely explanation: the minority impressions are proofs pulled directly from the plates, and therefore reversed, as a part of Rosenthal's normal proofing process; and the majority impressions are from an edition printed by offset and therefore not reversed from the image drawn on the plate. The artist needn't have been involved in the process. The production of mirror opposites was part of a normal job; the reversed proofs were not destroyed later because Gorky was used to working a composition both ways and did not see one orientation as necessarily better than its opposite.

26. The catalogue raisonné of Davis's prints by Sylvan Cole and Jane Myers (Fort Worth: Amon Carter Museum, 1986) does not mention his reversed proofs.

27. Another factor to consider is the extra cost for labor and press time to transfer to offset. Gorky was notoriously poor at this time, and it is unlikely that he had the money to print an edition, much less experiment with reversed impressions. Since these lithographs were made at the time of the Downtown Gallery's print exhibition, it is possible that the gallery, perhaps at the urging of Davis, covered the printing costs. The gallery's connections to Miller, via Davis, or Rosenthal, via Weber, make either shop a possibility.

28. Diane Waldman, *Arshile Gorky, 1904–1948: A Retrospective* (New York: Abrams, 1981), 28.

29. See Barbara Rose, *American Art since 1900* (New York: Frederick A. Praeger, 1967), 150.

Appendix

Following is a census of known impressions of Mannikin *and* Painter and Model, *organized by minority and majority orientations. As noted below, the present location of some impressions cited by Miller and Lader is unknown; in these cases data as to provenance, signature, numbering, and so on, are missing because such information is not available to the author. Measurements of impressions, which vary within a range of one to three millimeters because of uneven paper shrinkage, are not included. The description of impressions is limited to the several dark areas in each image where the most significant variations in printing occur.*

Mannikin (Minority Group)

1. Collection: Hans and Thordis Burkhardt
Provenance: Gift of the artist; illustrated by Miller
Unsigned, no date, number, or annotation
On proofing paper, oil stained, with mottled dark areas

2. Collection: Timothy Baum (cited by Lader, present location unknown)
Provenance: The Leonore Portnoff Collection, through Knoedler Galleries, 1973
Signed, Arshile Gorky (l.r.) and annotated "To my dearest Leonore"

Mannikin (Majority Group)

1. Collection: Art Institute of Chicago
Provenance: Onya LaTour, 1936, from Artists Union auction, 1936
Signed A. Gorky (l.r.) and dated 1936 in another hand, with additional notes verso in this same hand
On smooth wove paper, no watermark, oil stained, solid, flat dark areas

2. Collection: University of Michigan
Provenance: John Becker, 1948
Signed and dated (l.l.) A. Gorky, 1931, no number or annotation
On smooth wove paper with watermark FRANCE, with solid, somewhat shiny dark areas

3. Collection: Museum of Modern Art, New York
Provenance: Downtown Gallery, 1931; gift of Abby Aldrich Rockefeller, 1940
Signed Arshile Gorky (l.r), no date, numbered 23/25, and annotated "#2 Mannikin" in another hand
On smooth wove paper, no watermark, with solid, shiny dark areas

4. Collection: Whitney Museum of American Art, New York
Provenance: Ann Kendall, 1974
Signed Arshile Gorky (l.r.) and numbered 19/25, no date or annotation

On smooth wove paper with watermark *Rives*, with solid, flat dark areas

5. Collection: Sylvan Cole Gallery, New York
Provenance: Sotheby's, November 1989
Signed A. Gorky (l.r.), no date, number, or annotation
On smooth wove paper with watermark *France*, oil stained, with one solid, flat dark area

6. Collection: Marianne and Alan Schwartz
Provenance: Jack Rutberg Fine Arts
Signed Gorky (l.r.), no date, number, or annotation
On smooth wove paper, no watermark, with solid, shiny dark areas

7. Collection: Dave and Reba Williams, New York
Provenance: Christie's, May 1988
Signed A. Gorky (l.l), no date or number, annotated "To Mr. and Mrs. Graecen" (Albert Graecen was director of the Grand Central School of Art when Gorky taught there in the 1930s)
On smooth wove paper, watermark Rives, with solid, flat dark areas

8. Collection: Charles Collier
Provenance: Nina Perera (Nina Perera was special assistant to the WPA arts projects in Washington, D.C., in the early 1930s)
Signed A. Gorky (l.r.), no date, number, or annotation
On smooth wove paper, no watermark, with somewhat solid dark areas, retouched by hand

9. Collection: Dr. Robert Reiff (cited by Miller, present location unknown)
Provenance: From the artist to Mrs. David Metsger, thence to Reiff as a gift when he was preparing his dissertation on Gorky, and from his estate to a New York dealer (Miller mistakenly cited the Metsger and Reiff impressions separately, although Reiff in correspondence told her about the gift)

10. Collection: Saul Schary (cited by Lader, present location unknown)
Provenance: Cited in either the Whitney Museum Archives or the Archives of American Art

Painter and Model (Minority Group)

1. Collection: Dave and Reba Williams
Provenance: Christie's, January 1990
Signed A. Gorky (l.r.), no date or number, annotated "To Mr. and Mrs. Graecen"
On proofing paper, with mottled dark areas

2. Collection: Rona Benjamin (cited by Lader, present location unknown)
Signed A. Gorky, dated 1931, numbered 26/26

Painter and Model (Majority Group)

1. Collection: Brooklyn Museum
Provenance: Weyhe Gallery, 1964
Signed A. Gorky (l.r.), dated 1931 (l.r.), and numbered 8/25
On smooth wove paper, watermark *Rives*, with solid, flat dark areas

2. Collection: University of Michigan
Provenance: John Becker, 1948
Signed Arshile Gorky (l.r.), no date, numbered 16/25 (l.l.), annotated "#1 Painter and Model" in another hand
On smooth wove paper, no watermark, with solid, shiny dark areas

3. Collection: National Museum of American Art
Provenance: Mrs. Joseph Weiss
Signed A. Gorky, no date, number, or annotation
On smooth wove paper, watermark *Rives*, with solid, somewhat shiny dark areas

4. Collection: Newark Museum
Provenance: Charmion van Wiegand
Signed A. Gorky (l.r.), dated "1–31" (l.l.), no number or annotation
On medium smooth paper, no watermark, with solid, somewhat shiny dark areas

5. Collection: Worcester Art Museum
Provenance: Associated American Artists, 1990
Signed A. Gorky (l.r.), no date, numbered 5/25, no annotation
On smooth wove paper, watermark *Rives*, with solid, flat dark areas

6. Collection: Mooradian Collection
Provenance: Gift of the artist
Signed Arshile Gorky (l.r.), dated 1931, numbered 1/25

7. Collection: Dorothy C. Miller
Provenance: Probably a gift of the artist
Signed Arshile Gorky (l.r.), no date, numbered 12/25
On smooth wove paper, no watermark, with solid dark areas

8. Collection: William Muschenheim (cited by Lader, present location unknown)
Provenance: Kay Hillman

9. Collection: Mrs. Alexander Sandow
Provenance: Gift of the artist
Signed Arshile Gorky (l.r.), dated 1931 (l.l.), numbered 17/25, and annotated "To my friends Helen and Sandy"

10. Collection: Tom Weisel (cited by Lader, present location unknown)

Provenance: Knoedler Galleries

Signed Arshile Gorky (l.r.), dated 1931 (l.l.) and
numbered 1/25 (?) (Note: same number as impression in Mooradian Collection)

11. Collection:Descendant of a pupil of Gorky (cited
by Lader)

Provenance: Gift from Gorky to one of his students

Signed Arshile Gorky, no date, numbered 17/25
(Note: same number as Sandow impression listed
above), annotated to the pupil

On smooth wove paper, no watermark

12. Collection: Same descendant cited above

Provenance: Gift from Gorky to one of his students

Signed Arshile Gorky, no date or number

On smooth wove paper, watermark *Rives*

8 | THE LITHOGRAPHY UNIT OF THE FEDERAL ART PROJECT IN NORTHERN CALIFORNIA

JAMES WECHSLER

IT IS UNARGUABLE THAT DURING the Great Depression an overwhelming number of creative prints were made in New York City, where the workshop established by Graphic Arts Division of the Works Progress Administration, Federal Art Project (WPA/FAP) was responsible for the bulk of extraordinarily varied and innovative prints produced by the project during this time. The achievements of the New York workshop have so overshadowed the contributions of WPA/FAP printmaking in other regions of the country that little scholarly attention has been given to the project's accomplishments in these regions.

Printmakers on the New York City project were fortunate to have a well-established tradition of printmaking, as well as a structured system of museums, galleries, artists' organizations, and a nascent art press. This running start enabled the New York project to administer its printmaking division with comparative ease. Regions of the country that did not have a comparable infrastructure in place needed to build from the ground up.

In San Francisco, for instance, where Bay Area artists painted some of the first and most sophisticated frescoes for the Public Works of Art Project (PWAP) in the early 1930s, the graphic arts remained relatively unexplored. According to Joseph Danysh, regional adviser for the Federal Art Project in Northern California, one of the earliest functions of the Northern California project's lithography unit was to teach the process to artists: "[The] artists in California did not understand this medium when the Federal Art Project came into being."[1] In addition to introducing a spectrum of techniques to artists who were unfamiliar with the lithographic process, the lithography unit provided opportunities for artists employed on the project to make as many lithographs as they wanted. A variety of programs designed to make lithographs accessible to the public were established in order to generate a broad base of interest in prints.

The San Francisco lithography unit began operating in late 1935. Danysh's assistant, William Gaskin, has suggested that in the beginning the motive for establishing the unit was merely to handle the overload of artists who applied for the project. Not every artist could be commissioned to paint murals or design monumental sculpture or even to work at home without project supervision. "For these artists," he recalled, "we established a lithographic department." Although the lithography unit may have originated from these poor beginnings, it soon became an active and stimulating department within the Northern California project. According to Gaskin, the project produced a total of 52,000 lithographs between its inception at the end of 1935 and its deterioration in the early 1940s.[2] Gaskin's figure represents the total number of prints that were made available for allocation to various tax-supported institutions. Each stone was pulled in an edition of 28 impressions, which would mean the lithography unit produced roughly 1,850 editions.

The inspirational force behind the lithography unit was Ray Bertrand, a master printer who "was not only a competent lithographer but a sensitive artist in his own right, with the rare gift of knowing when to refrain from giving advice as well as when to give it."[3] Bertrand was teaching lithography at the California School of Fine Arts (now the San Francisco Art Institute) when Danysh and Gaskin approached him to supervise the unit and act as head printer. Bertrand's first task was to set up the unit in the project's headquarters at 1269 Turk Street. He did this by lending a number of his own presses to the project. Gaskin recalled that acquisition of additional presses proved challenging because it was then difficult to purchase a lithographic press that was not registered with the U.S. Treasury Department. Eventually the unit secured one through the Department of the Interior Parks Department.[4]

Commercial lithographers who applied to the project for employment were assigned to the unit. These experienced craftsmen put the project's leaders in contact with lithography houses that, suffering from the effects of the economic depression, were only too eager to sell the stones they had once used to print labels, decals, and advertising matter. Well trained in the traditional methods of lithography, the commercial men were responsible for grinding the old images off stones and preparing them for new ones. They assisted Bertrand in printing and also acted as advisers, instructing artists on the finer points of lithography.

Although this solved a number of immediate material and technical problems, it introduced some obstacles as well. As Gaskin remembered, there was often tension between the artists who wanted to experiment on the stones and the technicians whose "sensitivity as professional lithographers" would become "outraged" by undisciplined approaches to their craft. The artist Theodore Polos remembered that although Bertrand encouraged experimentation, "every time one of the commercial lithographers that were working with me saw what I was doing to the stone, they would tear their hair out." Aware of the potentially bad press that conflict between creative artists and curmudgeonly technical specialists might cause, administrators became watchful when hiring assistants for Bertrand to avoid "the undoubtedly competent and proficient, but militantly anti-modern" commercial lithographer "who inevitably winds up a choleric and heart-felt attack on `all this crazy stuff' by showing his portfolio of letter perfect cigar box ladies."[5]

Despite occasional clashes, however, the trained experts were put to good use in a group of portfolios that represented a genuine collaboration between artists and artisans. Related to work that was then commencing on the Index of American Design, two of these portfolios, "California Wild Flowers" by Alberte Spratt Lamb and "California Indian Petroglyphs" by Lala Eve Rivol, sought accurately to record and preserve aspects of the Northern California landscape. Permission was requested from the U.S. Forest Service to allow Alberte Spratt Lamb to take botanical specimens from forest lands so she could work from them in the project's studio in San Francisco.[6] A local authority on petroglyphs, Jack Greathead, was solicited by the project to escort Lala Eve Rivol to some of the most representative sites.[7]

Of these two portfolios, the petroglyph series was the more ambitious and in many ways the more valuable. In the words of Joseph Allen, state director of the Federal Art Project in Northern California, "the project was undertaken because the rock drawings were of artistic interest and it was hoped that the lithographic [sic] from them would be an influence in preserving the originals from vandalism."[8] A subunit of the lithography department was established at the onset of the FAP in December 1935 for the express purpose of making a portfolio that would include color plates and accompanying text describing the sites from which the images were taken. During the following two years Rivol visited various sites and made thirty-one detailed studies, twenty-six of which were translated onto stones by a lithographic draftsman who drew by hand as many as eleven color separations for each print.[9] In recognition of this cooperative effort, when the project was completed, Allen insisted that in catalogue entries, "credit for the lithography should go to Mr. [Fred] Bohne; the subject matter recorded as by Miss Rivol."[10]

In addition to these elaborate color lithography projects that involved a team of artists, draftsmen, and printers, the unit was responsible for a technical contribution that, in contrast to the labor-intensive color experiments, allowed scores of artists from all over the West to make original lithographs at a fraction of the usual cost for materials and labor. This development came in the form of a transfer paper that could readily be sent out to artists and later returned to project headquarters.

The paper was produced with relative ease, using inexpensive materials. It was first coated with a compound consisting of plaster of paris, flour paste, starch, and lead carbonate. Once this layer dried, the paper was steamed, placed face down on a lithographic stone, and run through a printing press. An impression of the stone's grainy texture was thus imprinted into the paper's coating, allowing artists to work on a surface that approximated stone.[11] Shortly after the paper was introduced, the critic Elizabeth McCausland enthusiastically observed that artists "working in Sacramento, Carmel and other outlying places, make their drawings on paper and send them to San Francisco to be transferred to stone and printed."[12] By September of 1937, in addition to receiving drawings from artists all over Northern California, Bertrand's unit had become responsible for printing transfer-paper drawings made by artists working on regional projects in Oregon, Washington, Nevada, New Mexico, and Arizona.[13] Within two short years, coming from a virtually nonexistent printmaking tradition, San Francisco established itself as a vital western lithographic center, far surpassing in scope and activity Southern California's lithograph unit, which had begun to operate out of Los Angeles in September 1936.

This rise of interest in lithography on the West Coast was not simply relegated to an artist-workshop relationship. Though the primary goal of the FAP was to preserve artists' skills and abilities by employing all artists who qualified for relief, it was also hoped that eventually the project would engender an enthusiastic, art-literate populace. Once it was clear that the lithography unit could indeed function effectively, Danysh arranged an experiment involving the Berkeley Public Library: lithographs from the project were loaned to anyone who wanted to borrow them. The Print Lending Project went into effect in November 1936 when twenty-five lithographs, including impressions from the petroglyph portfolio, were delivered to the library with the request that careful notes be kept concerning "the number of times they are loaned and the reception they receive," as well as "whether they are properly treated

and just how soon they become damaged."[14] All the prints were the property of the federal government; therefore when library patrons wanted to purchase them, it was recommended that they contact the artists to inquire whether any of the three impressions that the artists were allowed to keep for themselves might be for sale.[15]

With the expansion of the FAP's network of community art centers to Northern California, an effort was made to shift the concentration of prints from the urban center of San Francisco to outlying areas. As a result, when the Print Lending Project was discontinued in January 1938, the lithographs it had circulated locally went to fill the growing need for traveling art exhibitions on a regional and national level.[16]

By the early 1940s, as the FAP began to disintegrate, a significant project to promote lithography independently of the FAP was undertaken by Arthur Painter (the Northern California project's public relations man), the *San Francisco Chronicle*, and artists associated with the lithography unit. Perhaps as an attempt to wean artists from federal patronage, the *San Francisco Chronicle*'s Contemporary Graphics promotion offered readers a weekly selection of five original, signed lithographs, printed by Bertrand in editions of 140, that could be purchased for two dollars each through the newspaper or in certain department stores. The first five prints were reproduced in the paper on Sunday, 10 March 1940, accompanied by short biographies of the artists. During the ensuing weekdays, each of the prints was featured separately, along with a brief sales-oriented description. This offer was repeated each week, featuring works by different artists, until news of the growing war in Europe came to dominate the paper. The last lithograph appeared in the *Chronicle* on 5 April 1940.

Only through further investigation will

it be possible to chart the extent to which the revival of lithography in San Francisco under the FAP engendered the expanding interest in graphic art during the following decades. However, as Joseph Danysh said: "We who were in it and of it knew we were among the forefront of the people of that era who were extracting from the tragedy of the depression something beautiful and lasting."[17] Certainly their effort was great, and the contribution of the lithography unit was real.

NOTES

1. Joseph Danysh to Jane Isabel Curtis, Librarian, Alameda Free Library, 25 June 1937, Archives of American Art, Smithsonian Institution (hereinafter cited as AAA), microfilm reel DC59, frame 432.

2. William Gaskin, interviewed by Lewis Ferbrache, 28 February 1964, AAA, oral history project, reel 3419.

3. Joseph Danysh, "The Lithography Program of the Federal Art Project," manuscript submitted to *Prints* magazine (August-September 1936), AAA reel DC60, frame 217.

4. Gaskin interview, AAA, reel 3419. Gaskin said they received assistance from "someone connected with the Department of Interior—Parks Department"; presumably he meant the National Park Service.

5. Ibid; Theodore Polos, interviewed by Mary McChesney, 31 January 1965, AAA, oral history project, transcript; Joseph Danysh. "Lithography Program," AAA reel DC60, frame 217.

6. Joseph Allen to the U. S. Forest Service, Dept. of Agriculture, 20 February 1937, AAA reel DC59, frame 45.

7. Allen to Danysh, 12 February 1938, AAA reel DC65, frame 1070.

8. Ibid.

9. Danysh to Emanuel M. Benson, Editor of FAP Publications, 15 January 1937, AAA reel DC59, frame 99.

10. Allen to Dorothy Collins, supervisor of the FAP in Northern California, 4 March 1937, AAA reel DC59, frame 168.

11. Joseph Danysh, "Lithography Program," AAA reel DC60, frame 218.

12. Elizabeth McCausland, "Lithographs to the Fore," *Prints* 7:1 (October 1936): 28. The sections of McCausland's article that deal with the Northern California project are encapsulated from Joseph Danysh's manuscript, AAA reel DC60. Danysh apparently gave his information to McCausland when the editors of *Prints* decided to run an expanded article on lithography.

13. Danysh to Buckley MacGurrin, District Supervisor of the FAP in Southern California, 21 September 1937, AAA reel DC59, frame 637.

14. Danysh to Susan T. Smith, Librarian, Berkeley Public Library, 10 November 1936, AAA reel NDA1, frame 753; Danysh to Smith, 15 January 1937, AAA reel NDA1, frame 755.

15. Danysh to Smith, 11 February 1937, AAA reel NDA1, frame 756.

16. Danysh to Smith, 7 December 1937, AAA reel NDA1, frame 758.

17. Joseph Danysh, "Federal Art; A Memoir of the Thirties," manuscript, AAA, Danysh papers.

9 | THE PRINTS OF
WILL BARNET

DAVID ACTON

WILL BARNET IS WIDELY ACKNOWLEDGED
as one of the most influential American
printmakers of the twentieth century. His
creative powers are matched by technical
versatility and innovation. A long and distin-
guished teaching career has brought him
honors from such organizations as the National Academy of Design and the American
Academy of Arts and Letters. Recently the
artist presented the gift of the complete oeuvre
of his graphic art to the Worcester Art Museum, including an impression of each of
nearly 220 prints executed in the course of a
career spanning more than sixty years. This
body of work includes a number of prints not
described in the catalogue raisonné of Barnet's prints published by Sylvan Cole in 1972,
or in succeeding addenda.[1] Among these
prints are unique impressions of works never
editioned and working proofs that offer insight into Barnet's creative process, thus contributing to our knowledge of his achieve-
ment as a printmaker. They include works in
a variety of printmaking media, relating to

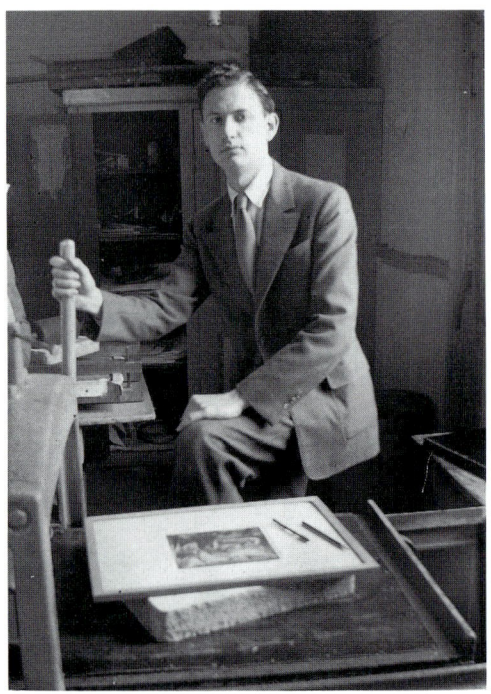

9.1 WILL BARNET at the Art Students League, 1937.

defining relationships of his subjects, including those shared with family members, friends, even pets. Over the years, Barnet's manner of representing these themes evolved from the specific to the sweeping, until in his late style, his art often reflects universal, spiritual concepts. This synopsis of the artist's career introduces thirty-one newly discovered prints, all of which are listed in the supplemental catalogue.

Will Barnet was born in 1911 north of Boston, in the coastal town of Beverly, Massachusetts. His father was a master mechanic and a lover of nature who kept a garden, a vineyard, and a house full of pets. The boy inherited his father's dexterity, and his own visual orientation drew him to art. When he was sixteen years old, Barnet began formal studies at the School of the Museum of Fine Arts, Boston, where he was the pupil of Philip Hale. In 1930 his success won him a three-year scholarship to study at the Art Students League in New York.

He was first drawn to printmaking at the league, where Charles W. Locke introduced him to lithography (figure 1).[2] The undescribed lithograph *New England Town* (supp. 1) would seem to have been produced in 1931 and may be his earliest surviving print. The artist brushed liquid tusche onto the stone in a tentative manner, as if experimenting with a new and unfamiliar technique. The casual, quickly sketched image represents the surroundings of Barnet's early years, a familiar subject that he might have rendered almost absentmindedly, when his goal was actually more technical. *Subway* (supp. 2; figure 9.2), another student lithograph, is more successful in its thoughtful composition and more commanding in its technique. Here Barnet sought to capture the fantastic space and eerie atmosphere that he found on a subterranean platform late at night. With its maze

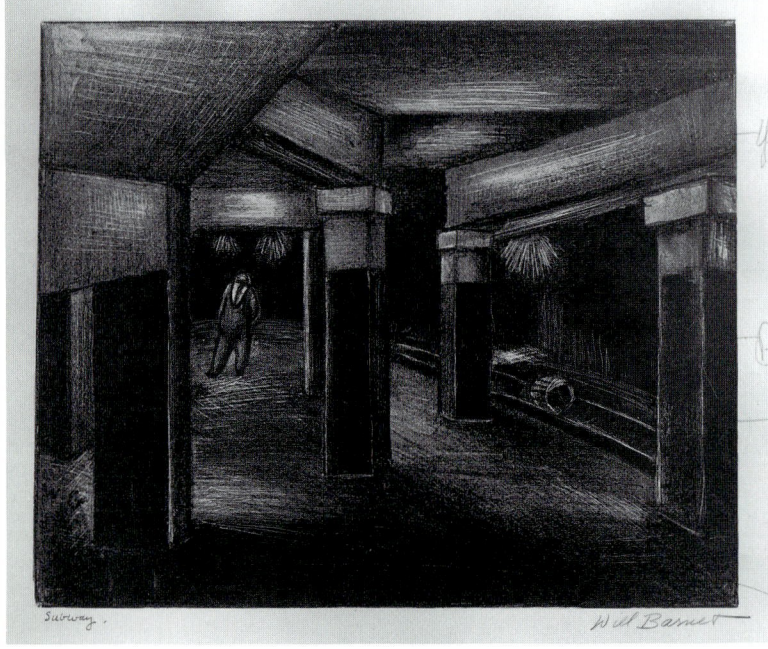

9.2 WILL BARNET. *Subway*, 1931. Lithograph. Supp. 2.

nearly all the stylistic phases of the artist's career, and reiterate the thematic evolution found in the rest of Barnet's sizable oeuvre. Most of his works represent deeply felt,

of eccentrically angled ceiling beams picked out in the dim light, the image borders on abstraction. A workman provides a reference for the scale and depth of the composition; his heedless retreat adds to the mood of loneliness. With crayon and liquid tusche the printmaker explored the tonal spectrum available in lithography, rendering passages ranging from silvery grays to saturated black; then, by scraping ink from the stone with a needle or knife point, he created other tonal effects and bright highlights. The Worcester impression of *Subway* has color notations penciled in the margins, suggesting that the artist contemplated transferring the design to a painting.

Locke, Barnet's teacher, was a methodical draftsman whose style combined the bravado of Honoré Daumier with the close observation advocated by the Social Realist painters, especially John Sloan, then president of the Art Students League. Barnet was encouraged by his teacher's example to continue his practice of using a sketchbook to keep visual notes on the habits and interactions of his neighbors. These influences are seen in Barnet's undescribed lithograph *The Concert*, which was probably made in 1933 (supp. 3; figure 9.3). On a bleak day two men sit on a stone bench in the park, their faces hidden as they huddle in thick overcoats. Though one plays the accordion for his companion, the music and friendship cannot soften the static composition and the somber mood of the image. This sullen theme reflects the disquiet of the Great Depression, also illustrated in Barnet's lithographs *Central Park Siesta* (Cole 1) and *Idle Hands* (Cole 28). The artist saw the city parks filled with unemployed workers, who alternated breadline stints with idle hours, bundled against winter cold and poverty. Their desperation is also found in the 1934 crayon lithograph *Cafeteria* (supp.

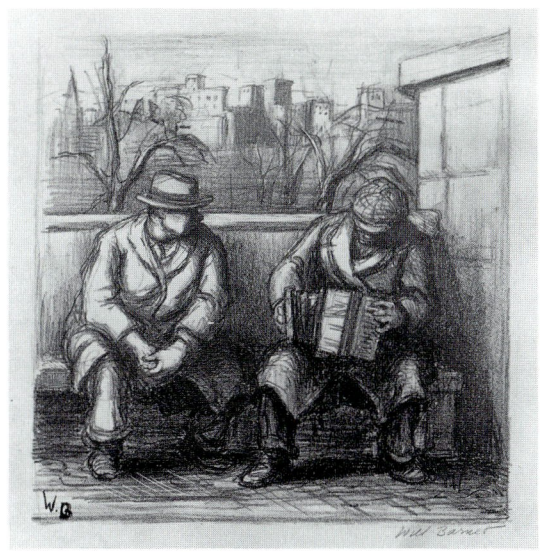

9.3 WILL BARNET. *The Concert*, ca. 1933. Lithograph. Supp. 3.

4), in which three men sit around a table in their coats and hats, with a single empty coffee cup before them. Scowls mask their faces, and the contrast between their inactivity and the surrounding restaurant bustle emphasizes their boredom and despondency. The style, technique, and imagery of this print are quite similar to Barnet's more congenial *Cafeteria Scene* (Cole 7).

By 1934 his outstanding capabilities as a craftsman secured Barnet a job as printer at the Art Students League. On the school presses he printed proofs and small editions from stones and plates prepared by the students. This position also made it possible for him to contribute to the government-sponsored WPA art program by printing for project artists on league equipment in his own time. In the following year Barnet joined the faculty, becoming the institution's youngest instructor of graphic arts. His prints at this time reflect the encouragement provided by this professional success, as well as by the continued nurturing support of his family. He drew constantly, depicting what he knew best and always imbuing his art with emotion.

9.4 WILL BARNET.
Portrait of Jeannette,
1938. Etching and dry-
point. Supp. 8.

9.5 WILL BARNET.
Father and Parrot, 1940.
Aquatint. Supp. 11.

In the etched portrait of his sister Jeannette (supp. 8; figure 9.4), executed in 1938,
Barnet experimented with Modernism. A
system of arching lines circumscribe and
facet form, evoking the vocabulary of Cubism.
The curves and repeated elliptical forms are
reminiscent of the work of Elie Nadelman
and Alexander Archipenko, and of the prints
of Henri Matisse. A few spare lines in the
background fracture space and push the figure close to the picture plane. In the area of
the sitter's forearm and collar, a web of soft
gray lines is just visible, showing where
hatchings of drypoint were burnished from
the plate as the artist adjusted his composition. Jeannette's distinctive facial features
seem quiet, assured, and confident, and her
expressive hands imply an unveiling of her
personality. This economical linear style is
also found in *The Loving Couple* (supp. 7), a
drypoint that is comparable to Barnet's more
resolved intaglio *Love Affair* (Cole 18). The
former print is accompanied at Worcester by
its preparatory design in pen and black ink on
a sketchbook leaf. In its pentimenti and era-
sures, the drawing shows how Barnet worked
out the composition and then transferred it to
the copper plate in sure drypoint lines. Passages shaded with wash became soft clouds
of aquatint on the plate.

Barnet's first one-artist show was mounted
at the Hudson Walker Gallery in New York
in 1938; soon thereafter he began teaching at
the New School for Social Research. In New
York printmaking was then perceived as mere
craft, subordinate in its creative and technical
demands to painting and sculpture. Prints
were difficult to exhibit and nearly impossible to sell. With admirable success, Barnet
transferred his primary attention to painting
and its instruction. However, several undocu-
mented printmaking experiments reflect his
inclination to make use of printmaking as a

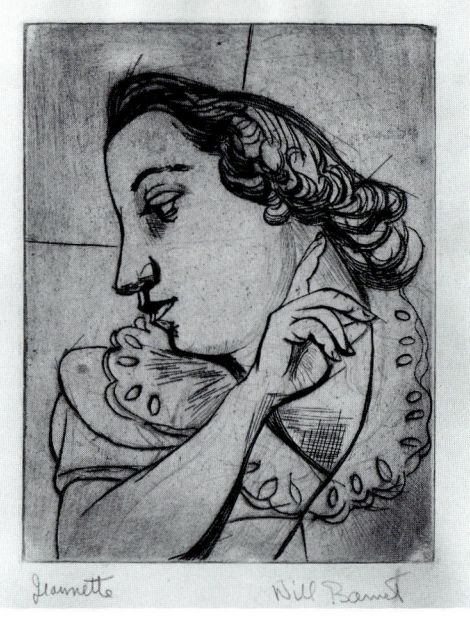

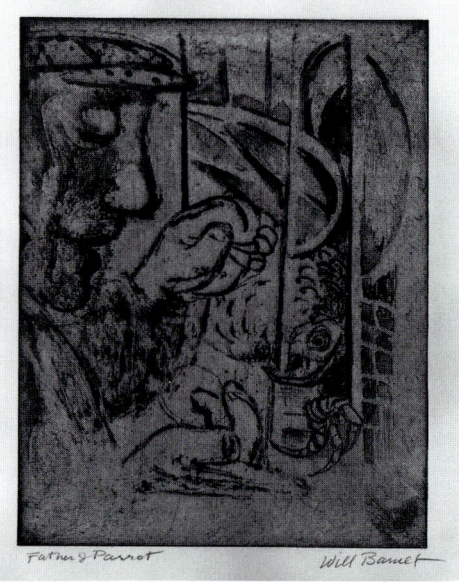

creative process and the artist's urge to keep
his hand in. Six incidental, undescribed plates
executed between 1938 and 1941, which represent the artist and his family, were not
printed in editions. One of these was the lift-
ground aquatint *Father and Parrot* (supp. 11;
figure 9.5), probably made in 1940. The shal-

low, uneven biting of the aquatint must have prompted Barnet to abandon the plate, which nevertheless remains articulate in its energy and emotion. The artist still owns a drawing in colored crayons that represents another version of this composition and was undoubtedly made in the preparation for the print.[3] Noah Barnet, and the pet bird he had acquired from a sailor lately arrived in New England from the South Seas, also appear in a woodcut variant of the present composition (Cole 52). In the drawing the parrot is upright, but in the print it is upside down, performing gymnastic flips in response to its owner. One can imagine cajoling phrases spoken to prompt the bird's excited reactions. The curling beak and talons echo the contours of half-folded wings to emphasize the parrot's acrobatics. With expressive, unfurling fingers the artist's father tempts his pet with crackers in a gesture similar to that in *Portrait of Jeannette.*

Several drypoints explore private, quiet moments in a hectic family day in Barnet's New York apartment. *A Moment's Rest* (supp. 12) depicts Barnet's wife taking a solitary break in her kitchen. In the drypoint *Mother's Bedroom* (supp. 10), she is joined by a child on his tricycle. Another tiny plate, representing the artist's wife and infant son, was used as a Christmas card in 1938 (supp. 9). Similar homey imagery appears in a pair of experimental aquatints made in 1940 and 1941, depicting the artist's children at the lunch table (supp. 15)or gazing dreamily out an apartment window (supp. 13).

The drypoint *At the Kitchen Table* of about 1940 (supp. 14; figure 9.6), which represents Barnet's son and his wife, pregnant with their second child, is remarkable for its psychological crosscurrents. The boy looks expectantly at his mother, brimming with precocious energy that contrasts with her exhaustion. She

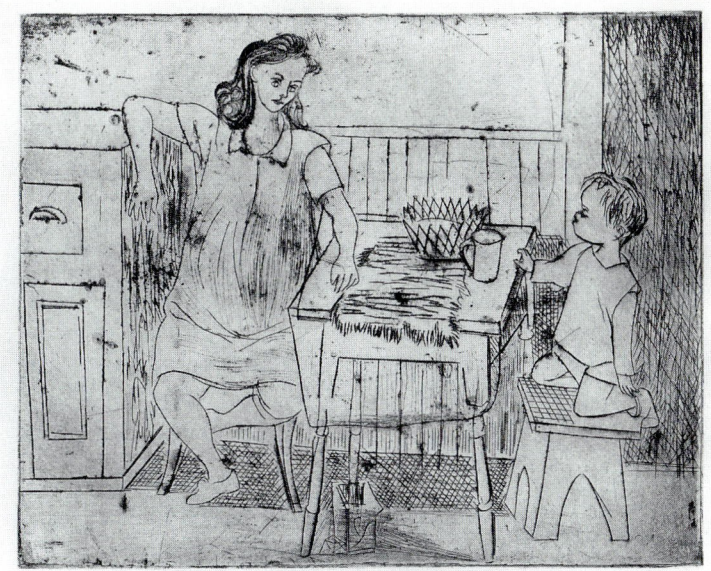

glances up with a look of perturbed acceptance, seemingly directed at the artist—perhaps suggesting her annoyance that his compulsive drawing has caught her at this awkward moment. This reminder of Barnet's presence also completes the family circle. The overall effect of the print is cozy and evocative, calling up memories of the inconsequential but fulfilling moments in all our lives. It is similar to the unguarded intimacy that Barnet observed and admired in the work of Matisse. Foul biting, fingerprints, and ink smudges on the Worcester proof of *At the Kitchen Table,* as well as such unresolved details as the table legs visible through a transparent cloth, show that the artist abandoned the plate quite early.

In 1941 Barnet made two remarkable drypoint self-portraits (supp. 16, 17), which show him seated, drypoint needle in hand, glancing up at his reflection with a look of rapt concentration. Perhaps a hint of a father's weary responsibility can be detected in his face. The technique of the larger print (supp. 17; figure 9.7) is particularly effective. Instead of single contour line, Barnet used bundles of microscopic needle strokes, overlaid and twisted in ropelike coils. In addition to outlining the figure, they model and imply form, with a nervous vacillation similar to a brushed ink line. For its rich plate tone, inky wiping, and the pits and blemishes that contrast with the delicacy of the drypoint line, the unique impression of this print is a connoisseur's delight.

In 1945 Barnet began teaching at Cooper Union, and the following year he relinquished his position as instructor of graphic arts at the Art Students League to teach painting instead. His wide circle of fellow artists exposed Barnet to new concepts, images, and styles, and he was increasingly drawn to abstraction. Late in the decade he was one of a group now known as the Indian Space Painters. These artists incorporated ideas from the European Modernism of Paul Klee, Pablo Picasso, and Hans Hofmann with similar concepts found in Native American art, especially that of the tribes of the Northwest Coast.[4] The New Yorkers were especially interested in the treatment of space by traditional artists who remained unaware of illusionistic, linear perspective. The Indian artists did not determine scale by spatial position, nor did they insist on clear distinctions between figure and ground, preferring to merge these forms in integral ornamental patterns. Like Cubism, this style favored compound views of a single object, melding elements of different points of perception in one quintessential form. The Indian Space Painters created designs that were flat and schematic, often incorporating an animal motif and exaggerating the beast's most distinctive features. Soon after the group began to exhibit together in 1946, Barnet joined them, having already incorporated the influence of Indian space into his own paintings.[5]

Few of Barnet's prints reflect the style and imagery of the Indian Space Painters. An ex-

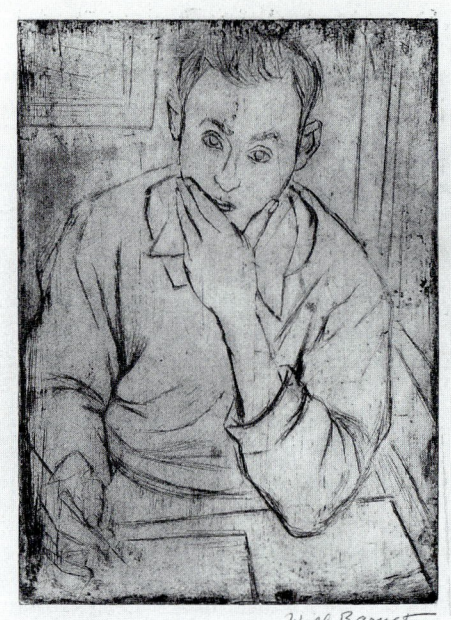

ception is the lithograph *Strange Birds* (Cole 93), which was based on one of the artist's first paintings in the style. This print is well known because its relatively large edition was published in 1947 by Chris Ritter of Laurel Gallery in his *Portfolio No. 1*. A newly discovered intaglio print that also reveals that style is *Rooster and Child* (supp. 24; figure 9.8). Characteristically, its semiabstract design combines animal and human motifs. The dominant rooster is a figure assembled from composite views. The static, frontal position of his body projects a mood of robust defiance, stabilized by outspread wings seen from above, while a side view of the head emphasizes the distinctive, exaggerated cockscomb and wattle. The cockerel's position, as he straddles a rotund, downy chick, may be for the protection of this offspring, who is contained in an egg-shaped capsule evoking the cycle of life. Standing next to the rooster is a man, of comparable scale, presented in a frontal, iconic pose. He holds a smaller figure before him, identified as an infant by outstretched hands and a swaddled body.

Stylized insects, each hovering in its own cell, underscore the theme of this image as the creatures' coexistence in nature. This style and imagery appear as well in the undescribed prints *Child and Cat* (supp. 22), *Girl and Cat* (supp. 23), and *Rooster and Cat* (supp. 25).[6]

Among the artists who influenced Barnet during the 1940s were his own children. With his encouragement, they would draw and paint for hours, and he was struck by the clarity and expressive power of their work. Sharing artistic experiences and images helped Barnet preserve the bonds with his young sons over a difficult time in his marriage, which ended in divorce in 1952. At about that time, Barnet returned to printmaking, which provided engaging technical challenges and the camaraderie of collaboration. In 1949 he and John von Wicht provided financial assistance to their mutual friend Robert Blackburn to help him open a printmaking workshop in Manhattan.[7] This studio was one of the first to make professional equipment and technical expertise available to a wide range of artists who wished to make prints; it continues to do so today. Together these artists experimented with color lithography and from 1949 to 1952 printed about twenty editions of Barnet's prints. Among them were the undescribed and uneditioned prints *Family Scene* (supp. 26), *Three Portraits* (or *Child with Cat and Bust*; supp. 27), and *Summer Sun* (supp. 28).

Another interesting image related to this activity is *Two Figures in a Garden* (supp. 29; figure 9.9), an uncompleted color lithograph executed in 1952. Barnet drew with pastels on this proof, printed only in green and light blue, demonstrating how he progressively planned the colors for these florid, complex lithographs, some of which used up to fifteen colors and were printed from as many stones.[8] The use of pastel also gives us some insight

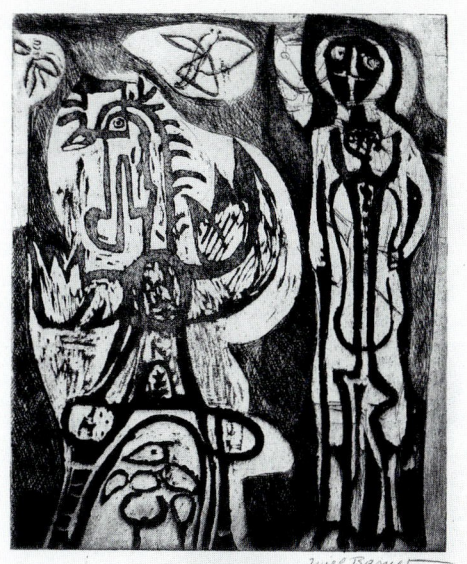

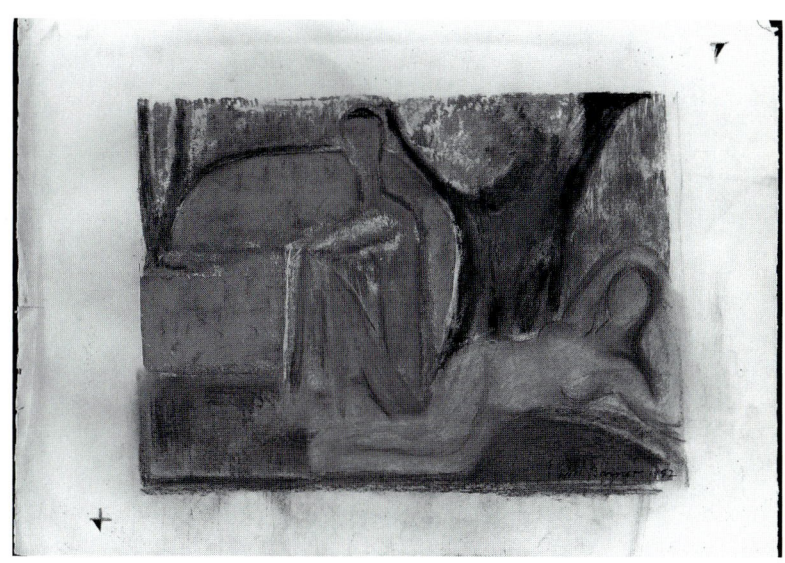

into how he arrived at the luminous, iridescent palette of many of these lithographs. Its style incorporates the influence of children's art; it is also typical of this period in its subject, which represents figures in a lush park or garden—imagery reminiscent of Pierre Puvis de Chavannes or Arthur Bowen Davies.

Beginning in the late 1960s Barnet perfected a figural manner that combined and distilled all his foregoing personal styles; this

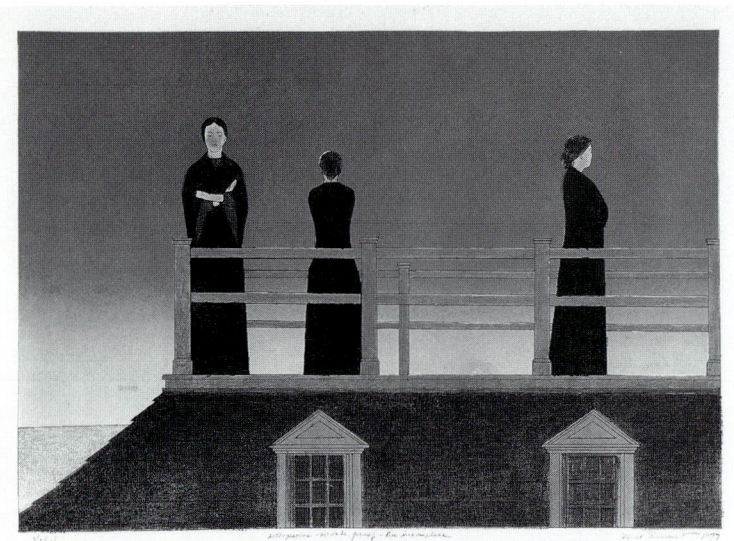

9.10 WILL BARNET. *Vigil,* ca. 1976. Lithograph. Supp. 31.

Maine.[9] One evening, the artist came upon his wife wrapped tightly in a shawl, silhouetted in the gloaming twilight, gazing at the sea. This haunting image became the leitmotif for several works that explored the historical, creative, and emotional heritage of New England, to which Barnet felt a strong link.[10] The finely tuned compositions not only create a placid mood, but also evoke our own contemplation of the individual's place in the vast world. For these images Barnet wished to create expansive settings to juxtapose with his meticulously drafted foreground passages of crayon work. To suggest limitless space, he used the device of aerial perspective. In *Vigil* this effect was achieved with a rainbow roll that gradually melded three different hues of blue-gray to depict the lightening sky near the horizon. He was unable, however, to achieve the exacting technical goals that he sought in this lithograph at such a distance from the Boston workshop. Thus he decided not to continue the print beyond the stage represented by this proof. This aborted project demonstrates Barnet's uncompromising technical standards and shows how deeply the artist was involved in the making of his collaborative prints. A similar struggle is represented by the 1975 color lithograph *Dawn* (Cole 157), which was begun with one lithographer and eventually editioned by another printer who was more responsive to the artist's wishes.

has become the art for which he is best known. Solemn in their mood and general rather than anecdotal in subject, these images were nearly always derived from finished paintings. The prints were generally produced in collaboration with master printers and were issued by several different publishers. Although the subjects are seldom identified, most of these prints represent Barnet's second wife Elena Chiurlys—whom he married in 1953—or their daughter, Ona. The later prints are well catalogued. Just one undescribed piece has been found, *Vigil* (supp. 31; figure 9.10), a color lithograph based on an oil painting of 1974. Barnet made this print in about 1976 at Impressions Studio in Boston in collaboration with master printer Paul McGuire. The impression at Worcester is designated "Lithographic work proof," and is probably one of just a couple of examples. The imprecision of its drawing and registration differs from Barnet's other, very meticulous prints of the period.

Vigil depicts a favorite subject of this time, which grew from a single experience. In 1971 the Barnets rented a seaside summer house in

Will Barnet's compulsive, yet delighted, involvement with technique is one of the notably consistent characteristics that emerges from his newly discovered prints at the Worcester Art Museum. These works also show how throughout his long career, heartfelt emotions were the true subjects of his art. They remain so today.

Many have been generous with their efforts and information in the organization of the Barnet print archive at the Worcester Art Museum and preparation of this article. I am grateful to Sylvan Cole, Bob Yahner, Susan Teller, and especially to Elena and Will Barnet.

1. Una E. Johnson and Jo Miller published the first extensive catalogue of Barnet's graphic art, *Will Barnet Prints, 1932–1964*, exhibition catalogue (Brooklyn: Brooklyn Museum, 1965), one in a series of monographs on American artists, published with support from the Ford Foundation. Nearly a decade later, Sylvan Cole compiled the definitive catalogue of Barnet's prints, *Will Barnet: Etchings, Lithographs, Woodcuts, Serigraphs, 1932–1972* (New York: Associated American Artists, 1972). Cole's catalogue included an introduction by Robert M. Doty, who later wrote a monograph on Barnet's paintings, *Will Barnet*, with an introduction by James T. Flexner (New York: Harry N. Abrams, 1984). In 1979, Cole published a supplement to his catalogue raisonné of the prints, extending its numeration from 148 through 168. Although there is no comprehensive catalogue of the artist's later prints, sixteen are described in the exhibition catalogue *Will Barnet, Master Prints 1979–1991*, with an introduction by Jan Garden Castro (Saint Louis: Jo Ann Perse Gallery, 1991). The Worcester Art Museum also owns impressions of all the prints of the 1980s and 1990s, which are beyond the scope of this article.

2. In many ways Locke's earlier experiences were parallel to Barnet's. After studying lithography at the Mechanic's Ohio Institute in Cincinnati, he went to New York in about 1923, where he attended classes at the Art Students League. Soon Locke was assisting Joseph Pennell with printmaking classes, and not long thereafter he took over the responsibilities of teaching lithography. See Clinton Adams, *American Lithographers: The Artist and Their Printers, 1900–1960* (Albuquerque: University of New Mexico Press, 1983), 50–51.

3. See Townsend Wolfe, *Will Barnet Drawings 1930–1990*, exhibition catalogue (Little Rock: Arkansas Art Center, 1991), cat. no. 13.

4. See Sandra Kraskin and Barbara Hollister, *The Indian Space Painters, Native American Sources for American Abstract Art*, exhibition catalogue (New York: Sidney Mishkin Gallery, Baruch College, City University of New York, 1991).

5. Ibid., 11. Peter Busa, one of the leaders of the group, had been Barnet's friend since their student days at the League in the 1930s.

6. The *Laurel Portfolio No. 1* also included prints by Joan Miró, Anne Ryan, Stanley William Hayter, Walter Pach, Reginald Marsh, and George Constant. A working proof of *Child and Cat*, with changes sketched in lithographic crayon, was included, with the same title in the Arkansas Art Center exhibition of Barnet's drawings; see Wolfe, *Will Barnet Drawings*, no. 24. The prints *Girl and Cat* and *Rooster and Cat* are similar to Howard Daum's *Cat and Bird*, a 1946 woodcut that was used for the cover of the first issue of *Iconograph* magazine, a short-lived, artist-run journal that explored philosophical, linguistic, and artistic facets of Native American culture. Daum had been Barnet's student at the league. See Ann Eden Gibson, "Iconograph Magazine," in Kraskin and Hollister, *Indian Space Painters*, 34–37.

7. For Blackburn's Printmaking Workshop, which is still in operation, see Elizabeth Jones, "Robert Blackburn: An Investment in an Idea," *Tamarind Papers* 6 (winter 1982–83): 10–14.

8. For a technical discussion of the color lithographs printed by Blackburn for Barnet and von Wicht, see David Acton, *A Spectrum of Innovation: Color in American Printmaking 1890–1960*, exhibition catalogue (New York: W. W. Norton and Worcester Art Museum, 1990), 184, 196.

9. See Doty, *Will Barnet*, 111–28.

10. This impulse is also reflected in Barnet's interest in Emily Dickinson, which inspired a series of drawings that often feature the silhouetted woman; see *The World in a Frame*, with poems by Emily Dickinson, drawings by Will Barnet, and an introduction by Christopher Benfey (New York: Abrams, 1989).

A Supplemental Catalogue

All measurements are in centimeters, height preceding width. The dimensions of the image or platemark are followed by those of the sheet. Worcester Art Museum accession numbers are in brackets.

1. *New England Town*, ca. 1931, lithograph on cream Rives BFK wove paper, 22.0 x 28.1; 29.0 x 40.3 [1994.279].

2. *Subway*, 1931, lithograph on cream Navarre wove paper, 23.1 x 22.4; 31.4 x 43.8 [1994.3].

3. *The Concert*, ca. 1933, lithograph on cream Navarre wove paper, 25.0 x 24.9; 31.0 x 48.0 [1994.6].

4. *Cafeteria*, 1934, lithograph on cream Navarre wove paper, 39.7 x 28.7; 48.6 x 31.6 [1994.7].

5. *Portrait of Mary*, 1936, color monotype on cream Japan paper, 40.6 x 29.5; 43.8 x 31.0 [1994.44].

6. *Portrait of a Woman*, 1936, color monotype on cream Rives BFK wove paper, 43.5 x 38.2; 51.9 x 40.6 [1994.45].

7. *The Loving Couple*, ca. 1938, drypoint with aquatint on white Rives BFK wove paper, 17.6 x 25.1; 25.3 x 32.0 [1994.4].

8. *Portrait of Jeannette*, 1938, etching and drypoint on cream Rives BFK wove paper, 20.1 x 15.0; 29.0 x 20.3 [1994.69].

9. *Mother and Child*, 1938, drypoint on cream Rives BFK wove paper, 11.3 x 7.5; 14.8 x 20.7 [1994.66].

10. *Mother's Bedroom*, ca. 1939, drypoint with graphite on cream Rives BFK wove paper, 25.0 x 19.9; 32.4 x 26.3 [1994.70].

11. *Father and Parrot*, 1940, aquatint on white Arches wove paper, 29.9 x 22.6; 37.6 x 33.2 [1994.59].

12. *A Moment's Rest*, 1940, etching and drypoint on cream Rives BFK wove paper, 17.4 x 20.2; 20.3 x 28.9 [1994.86].

13. *At the Window*, ca. 1940, aquatint on cream Rives BFK wove paper, 17.3 x 15.9; 32.0 x 24.2 [1994.103].

14. *At the Kitchen Table*, ca. 1940, etching and drypoint on white Rives BFK wove paper, 19.9 x 25.1; 31.6 x 40.3 [1994.84].

15. *Eating a Sandwich*, 1941, aquatint on cream Rives BFK wove paper, 22.7 x 27.5; 30.1 x 39.8 [1994.96].

16. *Self-Portrait*, 1941, drypoint on cream Auvergne wove paper, 16.7 x 12.4; 25.8 x 23.9 [1994.100].

17. *Self-Portrait*, 1941, drypoint on cream Auvergne wove paper, 24.9 x 17.5; 37.0 x 25.3 [1994.101].

18. *Child at a Table*, ca. 1942, aquatint on cream Rives BFK wove paper, 25.1 x 30.1; 29.0 x 40.4 [1994.102].

19. *Infant*, 1943, aquatint with etching on white Rives BFK wove paper, 22.3 x 34.9; 37.5 x 51.0 [1994.95].

20. *A Piece of Fruit*, ca. 1945, aquatint with ink wash on cream Rives BFK wove paper, 24.9 x 29.8; 32.1 x 41.7 [1994.109].

21. *Boy and Cat*, 1946, etching and drypoint with charcoal on cream Rives BFK wove paper, 20.9 x 28.4; 25.5 x 33.5 [1994.110].

22. *Child and Cat*, 1948, lithograph on cream Navarre wove paper, [24.1 x 33.8; 30.7 x 46.1 cm. 1994.111].

23. *Girl and Cat*, 1948, lithograph on dark cream Rives BFK wove paper, 48.4 x 58.8; 56.5 x 76.0 [1994.115].

24. *Rooster and Child*, ca. 1948, aquatint with drypoint on cream Rives BFK wove paper, 25.0 x 19.9; 32.0 x 25.0 [1994.117].

25. *Rooster and Cat*, 1949, etching and drypoint on white Arches wove paper, 20.0 x 24.9; 35.7 x 39.7 [1994.118].

26. *Family Scene*, ca. 1951, lithograph on cream Basingwerk Parchment wove paper, 25.0 x 41.4; 42.8 x 51.0 [1994.120].

27. *Three Portraits (Child with Cat and Bust)*, 1951, color lithograph on cream Rives BFK wove paper, 27.7 x 37.6; 40.8 x 57.6 [1994.132].

28. *Summer Sun*, 1952, lithograph on cream Basingwerk Parchment wove paper, 34.2 x 27.2; 48.1 x 33.4 [1994.141].

29. *Two Figures in a Garden*, 1952, lithograph with pastel on cream Rives BFK wove paper, 29.5 x 41.9; 40.4 x 57.9 [1994.142].

30. *The String*, 1953, color woodcut on cream Japan paper, 44.1 x 55.3; 47.0 x 63.8 [1994.143].

31. *Vigil*, ca. 1976, color lithograph on cream Arches wove paper, 53.3 x 74.4; 75.1 x 105.5 [1994.188].

10 | TWO LITHOGRAPHS BY

JOHN STEUART CURRY

SYLVAN COLE

IN 1976 ASSOCIATED AMERICAN artists published *The Lithographs of John Steuart Curry: A Catalogue Raisonné*, compiled and edited by Sylvan Cole, with an introduction by Laurence Schmeckebier, a Curry scholar and retired dean of the School of Art at Syracuse University. The catalogue lists and illustrates all forty-one lithographs known to its editor and to Kathleen Curry, widow of the artist.

Since publication of the catalogue, two additional lithographs have appeared. The more important of the two is a first stone of Curry's most famous lithograph, *John Brown*, drawn in 1939. Three impressions have been located, and each has an interesting history.

One, the printer's proof, bears a dedication in pencil, "John Brown for George Miller." This impression found its way from an estate auction to the Argosy Book Shop in New York City, and thence to Jane Allison of the Allison Gallery in Coventry, Connecticut. Dr. Allison sent the print for authentication to the director of the Cedar Rapids Museum

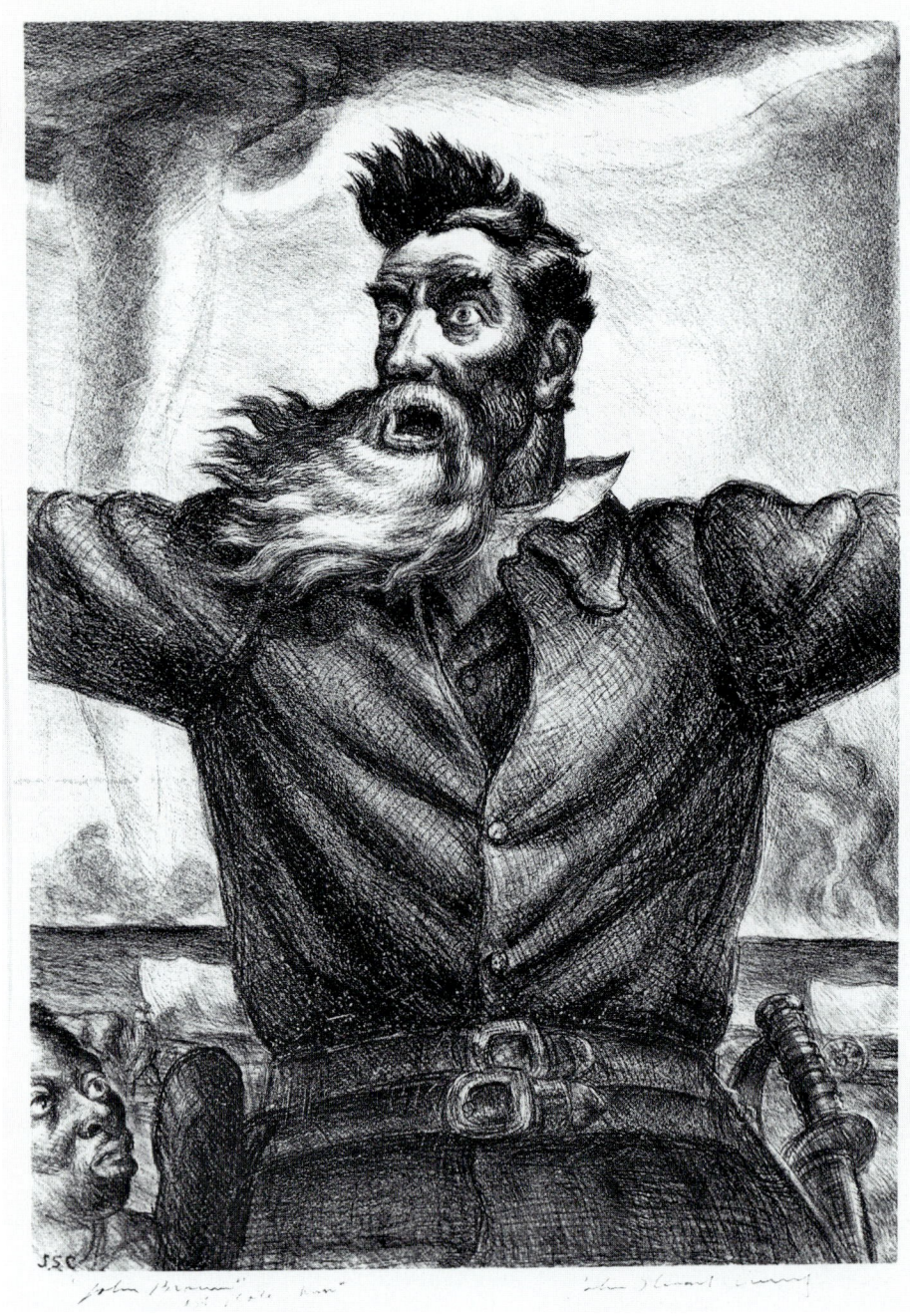

of Art, Joseph Czestochowski. There it was
lost and has not been seen since.

The second was in the collection of the
former Curator of Prints and Drawings at the
Cleveland Museum of Art, Leona Prasse (author of *Lyonel Feininger, A Definitive Cata-*

logue of his Graphic Work). Her estate sold
the print to Catherine Burns, a dealer in
Oakland, California, who in turn sold it to
the Sylvan Cole Gallery in New York. It was
leaning against a wall when Riva Castleman,
director of the Department of Prints and

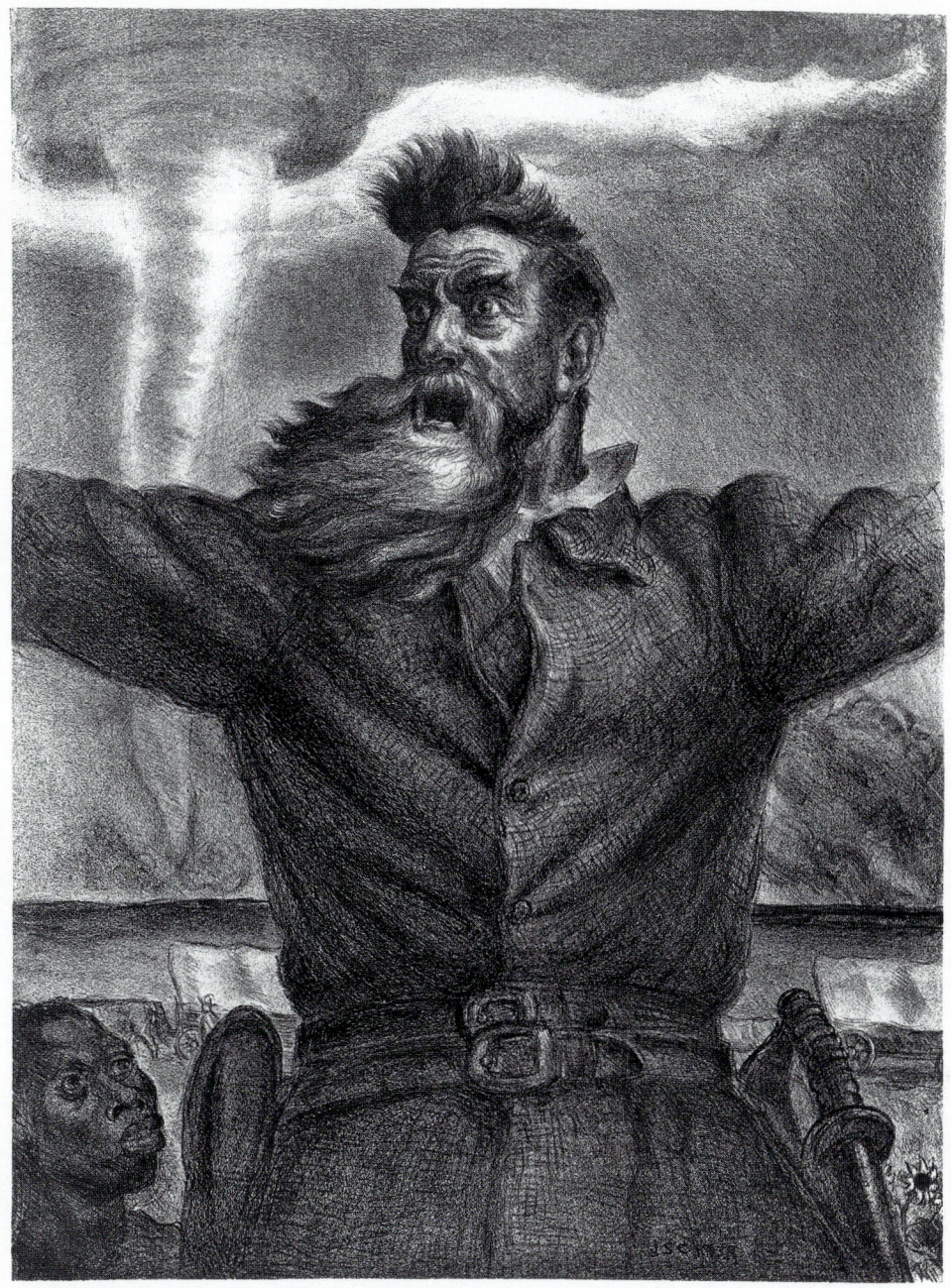

10.2 John Steuart
Curry. *John Brown,*
Second Version (Cole 34),
1939. Lithograph, 37.8 x
27.5 cm. Collection,
Tamarind Institute,
University of New Mexico,
Albuquerque.

Illustrated Books at New York's Museum of
Modern Art, visited the gallery. Very excited
by the print, Castleman acquired it for the
museum's permanent collection.

The third impression turned up in Rochester, New York, in the collection of Kathleen
Curry's daughter. Following her death, her
husband, Daniel Shuster, sold the lithograph
to the Elvehjem Museum of Art at the University of Wisconsin in Madison, where it
remains. Figure 10.1 is of that impression.

My conjecture is that either the stone

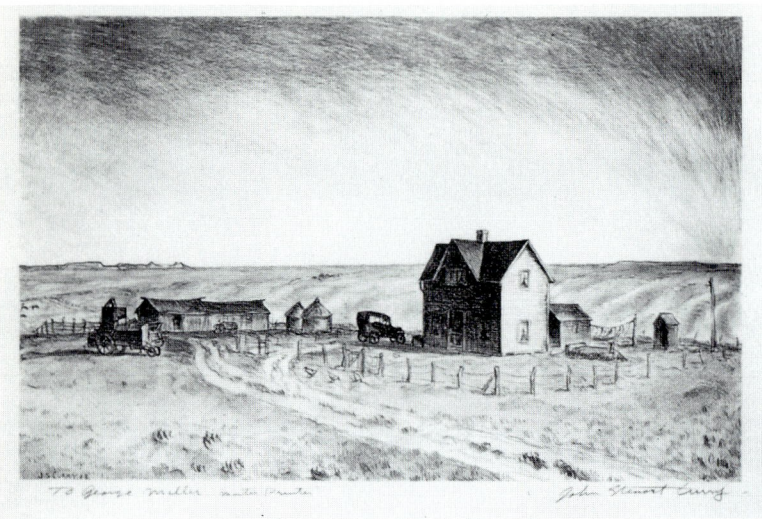

1. I am grateful to Jane Allison for providing a photograph of this lithograph. The impression formerly in her possession is dedicated "To George Miller master printer." It is now on loan from Steven Schmidt to the Spencer Museum of Art, University of Kansas at Lawrence.

10.3 JOHN STEUART CURRY. *Kansas Wheat Ranch* (or *Wheat Ranch Kansas*), ca. 1929. Lithograph, 22.7 x 35.2 cm. Private collection.

went bad after the three proofs were pulled, or that Curry was unhappy with the violence of this image and decided to draw a second stone, which was then printed in an edition of 250 published by Associated American Artists (figure 10.2).

The amendment to the catalogue raisonné should read:

34a *John Brown*, First Version, 1939.

Three known proofs, 14 3/8 x 10 in. (36.5 x 25.4 cm).

Initialed JSC in stone, lower left.

The other lithograph that has turned up is *Kansas Wheat Ranch* (figure 10.3). A larger version of Cole 7, same title, which measures 3 1/4 x 4 1/4 inches (8.1 x 10.6 cm), it was done ca. 1929 in a numbered edition of one hundred and used as a Christmas card.[1]

The amendment to the catalogue raisonné should read:

7a *Kansas Wheat Ranch* (or *Wheat Ranch Kansas*), ca. 1929.

Edition unknown, 8 15/16 x 13 7/8 in. (22.7 x 35.2 cm).

96

Sylvan

Cole

11 | THEODORE H. CUNO

(1877–1967)

CLINTON ADAMS

IN *AMERICAN LITHOGRAPHERS 1900–1960*, I provided a brief account of the work of Theodore H. Cuno, a skilled lithographic printer who was active in Philadelphia from 1912 into the 1950s.[1] As only fragmentary information about Cuno's work was then to be found in published sources, I based that account principally upon interviews with artists who had worked with him. I was then unable to locate the printer's surviving heirs; now, however, Charles K. Cuno, Jr., the printer's great nephew (who, through his father, inherited the printer's estate) has provided further information about the printer's life and work.[2]

Theodore Cuno was born in Germany on 1 March 1877. An unidentified journalist's interview (found in typescript among Cuno's papers) tells us that he studied lithography in Hamburg and printed in Bavaria before emigrating to the United States, apparently in 1912.[3] Upon arrival in Philadelphia he gained employment as a color-prover at the Ketterlinus Company, then located at Fourth and

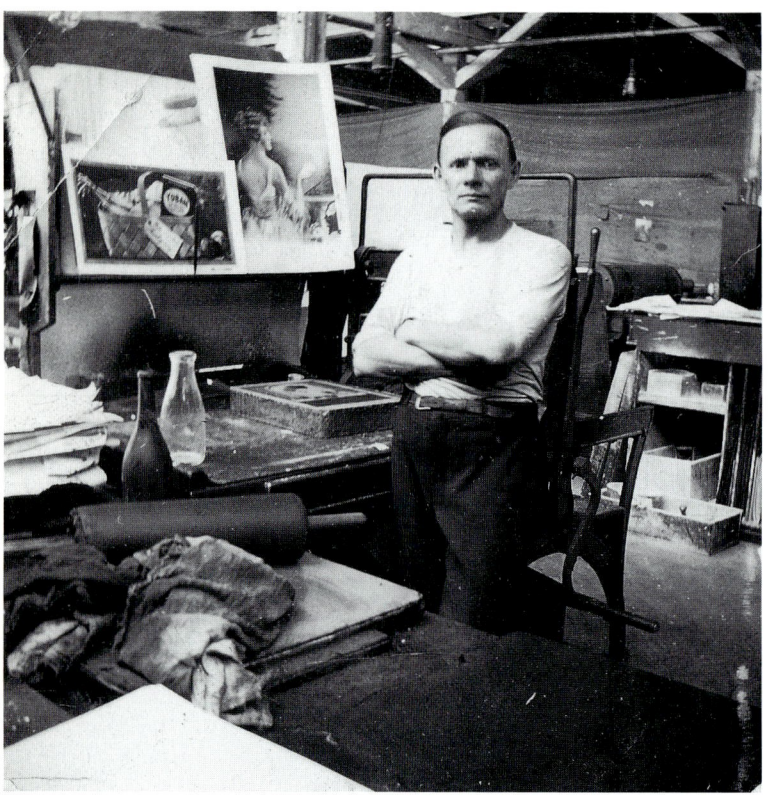

11.1 THEODORE CUNO
in the pressroom of the
Ketterlinus Company,
Philadelphia, ca. 1912.

Arch streets in Philadelphia. Carl Zigrosser
has written that Cuno worked with Joseph
Pennell, whose drawings of the Panama
Canal and of the American West were transferred and printed at the Ketterlinus Company in 1912.[4] Cuno also printed lithographs
for the Swedish-American artist Birger
Sandzen beginning in that year.[5]

While still working for Ketterlinus, Cuno
established (in or before 1931) a small shop in
the basement of his home at 7535 Lawndale
Avenue in Philadelphia, where he printed
lithographs for artists and illustrators.[6] For
a time, Cuno also printed on a press located
at the Print Club of Philadelphia on Latimer
Street.

Jerome Kaplan, for whom Cuno printed,
told me that, like other printers of his generation, Cuno "didn't offer any technical information" and that "he was very close-mouthed

about his technique." Others spoke warmly
about Cuno's collaborative skills: "He was
so enthusiastic, so warm, so friendly," Jack
Bookbinder said. "In working with him, one
felt it was a labor of love." Benton Spruance
called Cuno "a great printer, one of the best
in the country."[7] Never fluent in English (he
spoke with a pronounced German accent),
Cuno was devoted to his work, and appears
to have had few interests other than lithography and his family. He was married to
Margaret C. Cuno (d. 1951) and had two
daughters, Margaret and Johanna.

Cuno retired from the Ketterlinus Company in 1953.[8] In 1966, shortly before his
death on 18 January 1967 at the age of eighty-
nine, the printer gave his printing press, lithographic equipment, stones—many of which
still carried images—and a large number of
lithographs to his nephew Charles K. (Koppi)
Cuno, Sr., who, at his death in 1991, left
them to his son Charles K. Cuno, Jr.[9]

The younger Cuno has since moved the
printer's press- equipment to his home in
Swedesboro, New Jersey, and is endeavoring
to catalogue the lithographs. Although these
prints were stored for twenty-five years by
Koppi and Angeline Cuno in the attic of their
home, most are in good condition. Many of
the more than 2,000 prints (of approximately
750 images) are unsigned; some artists have
not yet been identified.

Following is a partial list of artists known
to have collaborated with Theodore Cuno:

Alfred Bendiner (1899–1964)
Julius T. Bloch (1888–1966)
Jack Bookbinder (1911–90)
John E. Costigan (1888–1972)
Jean Francksen (b. 1914)
Wanda Gág (1893–1946)
Maxim B. Gottlieb (b. 1903)
William Gropper (1897–1977)

Alexandre Hogue (1898–1994)

Peter Hurd (1904–84)

Cynthia W. Iliff (b. 1907)

Martin Jackson (b. 1919)

Jerome Kaplan (b. 1920)

Doris Lee (1905–1983)

William Libby (b. 1919)

Merritt Mauzey (1898–1973)

Joseph W. McDermott (dates unknown)

Henry C. Pitz (1895–1976)

Robert Riggs (1896–1970)

Raphael Sabatini (1896–1985)

Birger Sandzen (1871–1954)

Benton Spruance (1904–67)

Prentiss Taylor (1907–91)

Mildred E. Williams (1892–ca.1960)

Zsissly (pseudonym of Malvin Marr
    Albright, b. 1897)

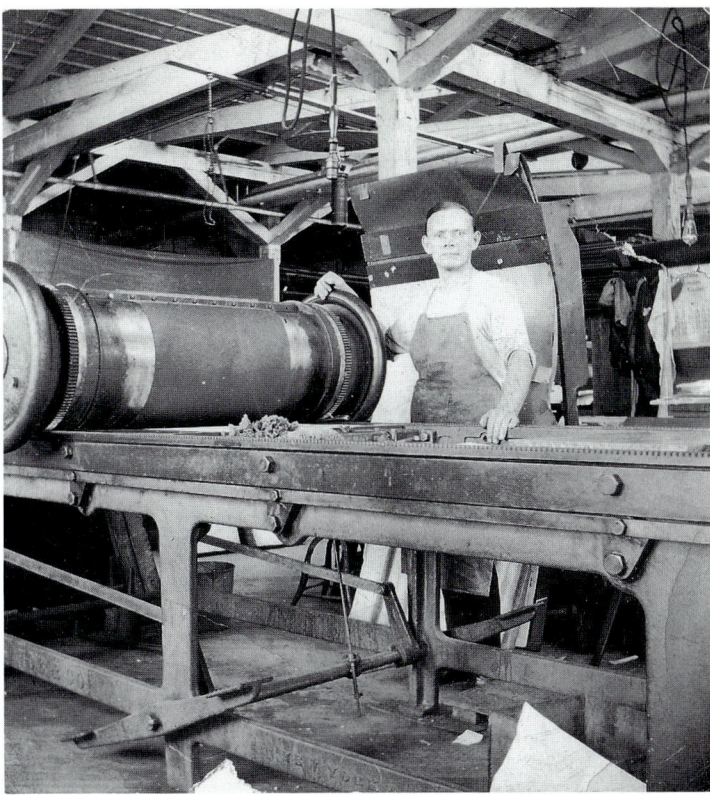

NOTES

1. Clinton Adams, *American Lithographers 1900–1960: The Artists and Their Printers* (Albuquerque: University of New Mexico Press, 1973), 115–18.

2. I am indebted to Charles K. Cuno, Jr., for much of the information upon which this note is based and for permission to reproduce the photographs of Theodore H. Cuno that accompany it. The "Cuno papers" cited in these notes are a sparse collection of notes, correspondence, clippings, and so on, inherited by Charles Cuno in 1991.

3. The undated typescript (signed "Jeanne") reads in part as follows:

> Back in 1912, a young German printer was invited to take a job in St. Petersburg in what was then Czarist Russia. The idea was interesting to Theodore Cuno, but his mother took a dim view of it. "You must not go," she protested, "They will send you to Siberia!"
>
> "Very well," said Theodore Cuno. "If I cannot go to Russia, I will go to the United States!"
>
> And that's how a woman's intuition saved a young man from bloody revolution and the chill confines of Communism—steering him instead

toward a position in a fine Philadelphia printing house and finally into a business of his own that brought him in contact with some of the leading artists in the United States (Cuno papers).

4. Carl Zigrosser, *Benton Spruance, Lithographs, 1932–67,* exhibition catalogue (Philadelphia: Philadelphia College of Art, 1967).

5. In a handwritten letter (possibly never sent) dated 29 December 1964, Cuno states that he worked with Sandzen in 1912 (Cuno papers).

6. Following the death of his wife, Margaret, in 1951, Cuno moved to 5908 Alma Street, Philadelphia, home of his daughter Johanna and her husband, Paul H. Williams, and again established a basement workshop. Following a family rift, Cuno returned to the Lawndale Avenue address, then the home of his sister Freida, where she and Angeline Cuno (wife of his nephew) cared for him until his death in 1967.

7. Kaplan to Adams, 21 May 1978; interview, Bookbinder with Adams, 9 May 1979; Cuno papers, "Jeanne," typescript.

11.2 THEODORE CUNO in the pressroom of the Ketterlinus Company, Philadelphia, ca. 1912.

8. Throughout his life, Cuno remained a member of Local 14 of the International Association of the Amalgamated Lithographers of America.
9. Charles K. Cuno, Sr. (1899–1991), who had learned lithographic printing in Hanover, Germany, sometimes worked with his uncle in Philadelphia as an assistant at the press.

12 | THE RUTGERS ARCHIVES

FOR PRINTMAKING STUDIOS

TRUDY V. HANSEN

THE EXPLOSIVE GROWTH OF AMERICAN printmaking workshops during the past thirty-five years has provided artists with an opportunity to work with an amazing range of talented printers and has led to a radically expanded definition and history of the contemporary print. Museums throughout the United States have begun to actively collect the prints produced in collaborative printmaking workshops, and many, recognizing the importance of this movement, have established archives to document the history of large and small workshops. Among the archives thus established are those of Cirrus Editions (Los Angeles County Museum of Art); Crown Point Press (Achenbach Foundation for Graphic Arts, Fine Arts Museums of San Francisco); Experimental Workshop (Santa Barbara Museum of Art); Gemini G.E.L. and GraphicStudio-South Florida (National Gallery of Art, Washington, D.C.); Landfall Press (Milwaukee Art Museum); Limestone Press (Stanford University

tute of Chicago). Most of these archives contain the work of a single printmaking studio.

By early 1982, Phillip Dennis Cate, director of the Jane Voorhees Zimmerli Art Museum at Rutgers University, recognized that the work of smaller shops was often relatively unknown and that many printers had neither the time, space, capability, nor inclination to maintain an archive and history of their production. Accordingly, he began to discuss with such printers the possibility that the museum might become caretaker to the histories of a select group of printmaking studios.

Later in that year, the Rutgers Archives for Printmaking Studios was established as a repository for prints and related preparatory materials from several printmaking workshops in the New York area. By 1994 the archives represented in depth the work of more than three hundred artists and twenty-two presses, and its holdings surveyed a broad spectrum of the trends, techniques, and artistic concerns of the past decade. In combination with hundreds of other prints collected individually from workshops and artists across the country since 1960, the Zimmerli Museum has developed a strong focus on contemporary American graphics and particularly on the projects of collaborative print workshops. While developing a nationally recognized collection that documents the collaborative efforts of master printers and the distinctive groups of established and emerging artists who work with them, the museum has simultaneously collaborated with printers and artists on a dynamic program of exhibitions, publications, and special projects.

The twenty-two presses represented in the Rutgers Archives (as of December 1994) included fourteen from New York: K. Caraccio Etching Studios, Condeso/Brokopp Studio, Derrière L'Etoile Studios, Chip Elwell, Grin

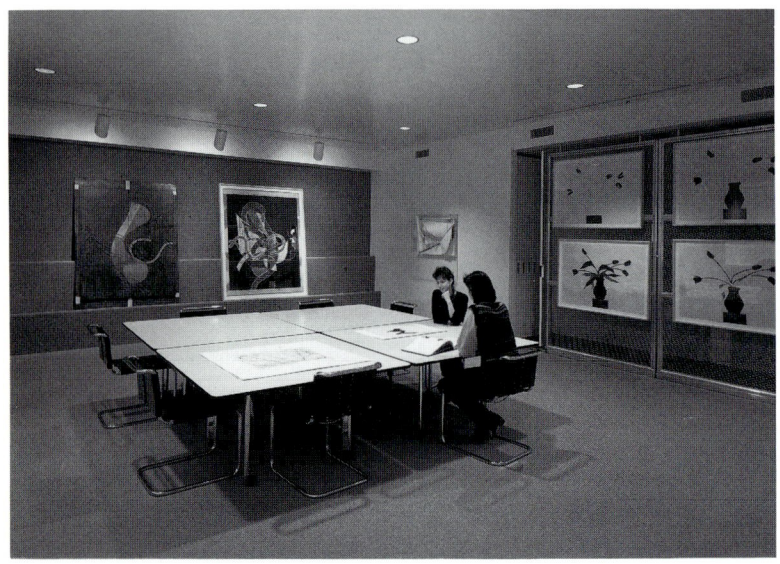

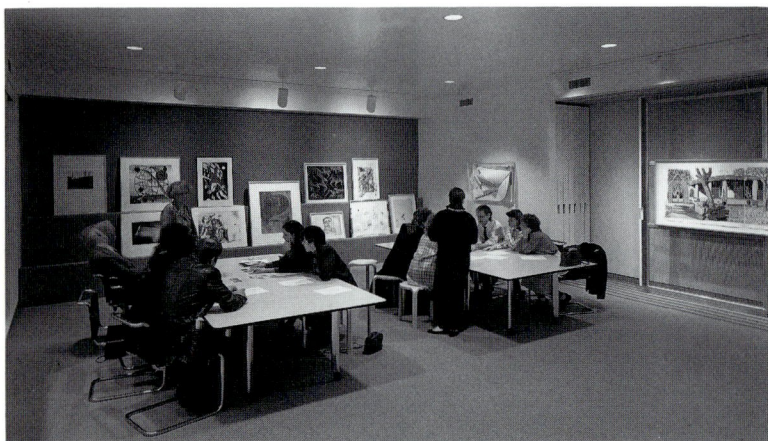

12.1 McKnight Print Study Room, Walker Art Center, Minneapolis. The Tyler Graphics archive includes many oversize prints; a system of pull-out racks (seen at right) houses large framed impressions. The combination of a multilevel, wall-display area and the pull-out racks assists the curators to prepare the room for varied uses by scholars and print-study groups.

12.2 McKnight Print Study Room, Walker Art Center, Minneapolis.

Museum of Art); Tamarind Lithography Workshop and Tamarind Institute (University of New Mexico Art Museum, Albuquerque); Tandem Press (Elvehjem Museum of Art, University of Wisconsin, Madison); Tyler Graphics (Walker Art Center, Minneapolis); and Universal Limited Art Editions (Art Insti-

102

Trudy V. Hansen

Graphics, Hudson River Editions, Lisa H. Mackie Studios, Maurel Studios, Catherine Mosley Studios, John Nichols Printmakers and Publishers, Pelavin Editions, Solo Impression, XPress, and Yama Prints; and eight from other states: Auclair Graphics (California), Echo Press (Indiana), Fox Graphics-Merrimac Editions (Massachusetts), made in California, Magnolia Editions (California), the Rutgers Center for Innovative Printmaking (New Jersey), Shark's (Colorado), and Teaberry Press (California). Almost two thousand prints and several thousand supplementary objects reflect the specialties and attitudes of a diverse group of printers, with prints ranging from the most traditional to those with the most innovative and complicated technical applications and solutions. The goal has been to acquire not only finished prints, but also to collect and exhibit the plates, blocks, preliminary drawings, proofs, test samples, and other types of materials that would help illustrate the technical and artistic evolution of print projects. As a university art museum with a primary function as a research center and teaching facility, the development of an in-depth collection in conjunction with a diverse group of master printers was seen as a mutually beneficial undertaking.[1]

As material began to be donated through the generosity of the presses, their artists, and a wide range of dealers and publishers, other benefits of the collaboration became evident. Permanent gallery space at the museum was allotted for the archives, and a series of special exhibitions and catalogues focusing on the methods of contemporary print production were mounted in 1988, 1989, and 1990. Symposia, workshops, tours, classes, and other programs regularly draw on the expertise of the participating master printers, and the work produced by each press is pub-

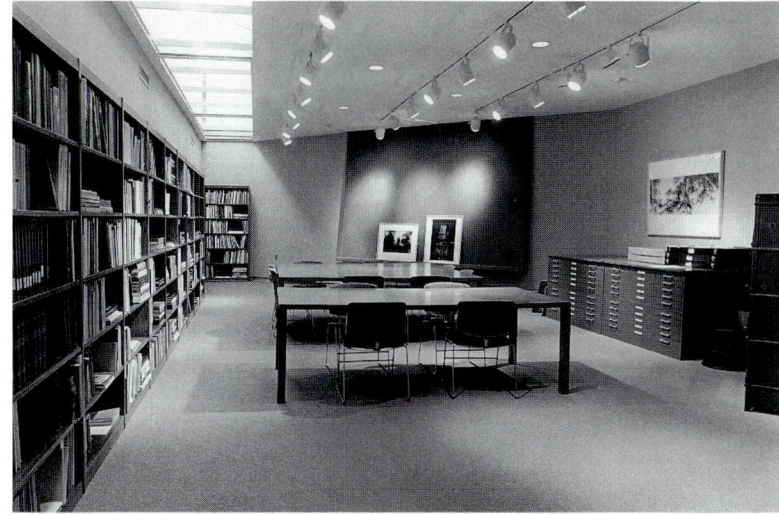

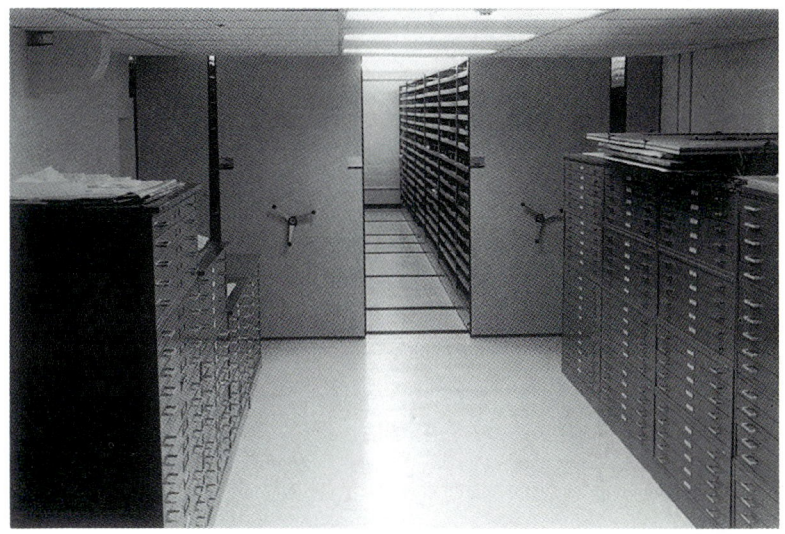

12.3 Prints and Drawings Study Room, The David and Mildred Morse Research Center for Graphic Arts, Jane Voorhees Zimmerli Art Museum, Rutgers, The State University of New Jersey.

12.4 Print storage facility, The David and Mildred Morse Research Center for Graphic Arts.

lished in fully illustrated checklists that have been widely distributed free of charge to museum and university libraries through the support of the National Endowment for the Arts.

As part of the continuing commitment to the forty-five thousand works on paper in the

Zimmerli's collection, a five-year expansion and renovation program was initiated in 1992. During the first stage of renovation, the museum's print storage facilities were upgraded and expanded, creating safer storage areas and easier access to the growing collections. The renovated David and Mildred Morse Research Center for Graphic Arts, opened in 1994, offers a new study room for prints and drawings, a rare book library, and offices and work spaces for the print department. Biographical files have been developed to help place specific prints within the context of an artist's overall body of work; other informational files allow study of the scope of the collaborative press movement in the United States. For researchers particularly concerned with printmaking processes, documentation sheets (prepared by the presses for each edition or unique work that is donated) are included in object files whenever possible. A small video library documenting printmaking techniques and collaborations at printshops is being developed, and information on new sources for films and videos is always welcome.

Perhaps the best-known activity of the Rutgers Archives is the annual portfolio subscription program. Each year, master printers who are members of the archives are invited to submit proposals for projects to be commissioned and published by the museum. While annual portfolios reflect a mix of established and emerging artists, projects involving artists who have worked primarily in other visual arts media and those utilizing new technologies, processes, and materials have been particularly encouraged. In addition to supporting the work of member presses, the program helps fund the continuing maintenance and exhibition of the collections, as well as the archives' publishing program. Since 1983, the Zimmerli Museum has pub-

lished more than forty editions that have been collected by museums, corporations, and individuals. The list of artists published is indeed eclectic and includes such artists as Terry Allen, Candida Alvarez, Jane Dickson, Mary Frank, Rupert Garcia, Lawrence Gipe, Joseph Goldyne, April Gornik, Yvonne Jacquette, Georgia Marsh, Melissa Miller, Miriam Schapiro, T. L. Solien, and William T. Wiley.

The Rutgers Archives for Printmaking Studios continues to evolve as a comprehensive resource for the study of contemporary printmaking and the collaborative artist-printer relationship. Future plans include the reinstallation of the museum's contemporary print galleries; funding is currently being sought for the production of an interactive video display that will help museum visitors understand printmaking techniques and the stages involved in the development and production of print projects.

Clearly, the body of work that is being preserved in the various archives of American printmaking studios can provide the visual substance for ever-expanding definitions and discussions of printmaking and prints by current and future generations. As dialogue proceeds with respect to technical and conceptual definitions of the original print and the blurring of boundaries between the visual arts and other art forms, these archival collections will provide indispensable documentary evidence to support scholarly research on printmaking in the late twentieth century.

NOTE

1. The Rutgers Archives are complemented by the Zimmerli Museum's outstanding collection of late nineteenth-century French prints, posters, books, and periodicals, including a specialized body of

Trudy V. Hansen

works of art on paper that illustrate the Western world's fascination with the art of Japan; a substantial number of plates, blocks, and other materials that demonstrate the evolution of print projects; and a wealth of research materials with respect to the operations and working relationships of the printers, publishers, and art dealers in France who produced and distributed countless editions of late nineteenth- and twentieth-century print and poster editions.

CONTRIBUTORS

DAVID ACTON, curator of prints and drawings at the Worcester Art Museum, was editor and principal author of *Spectrum of Innovation: Color in American Printmaking, 1890–1960* (1990). He has written extensively on individual American printmakers, most recently on the work of Gustave Baumann and George Miyasaki. He is currently occupied with organization of a comprehensive (and long overdue) exhibition of Abstract Expressionist prints.

CLINTON ADAMS, a painter, printmaker, and historian, has been associated with Tamarind since its founding in 1960. He established *The Tamarind Papers (TTP)* in 1974 and served as its editor until 1990. He is author of five books and more than one hundred articles and exhibition catalogues, principally on the history of American lithography. Most recent among these are a biography and catalogue, *Crayonstone: The Life and Work of Bolton Brown* (1993) and *The Drum Lithographs: 1960–1963* (1994).

PHILLIP DENNIS CATE became director of the Jane Voorhees Zimmerli Art Museum at Rutgers University in 1970; since then he has made printmaking his major focus and that of the Zimmerli. His areas of expertise are fin de siècle French graphic arts and Japonisme. In 1975 he co-organized with Gabriel Weisberg the exhibition *Japonisme: The Japanese Influence on French Art, 1854–1910;* later, he collaborated with the staff of the Bibliothèque Nationale on *Pissarro to Picasso, Color Etching in France.* Currently he is working on the exhibition and publication *The Spirit of Montmartre: Cabarets, Humor, and the Avant-Garde, 1875–1905.*

SYLVAN COLE, a specialist in American prints and drawings (1910–60) is director and owner of the Sylvan Cole Gallery in New York. As a dealer, he first worked with Associated American Artists in 1946; he became its director in 1958 and resigned to found his own gallery in 1983. He was one of the four founders of the International Fine Print Dealers Association in 1986 and was elected president of that 160-member organization in 1994. He has written catalogues raisonnés on Will Barnet, Stuart Davis, Joseph Hirsch, and Grant Wood, as well as on John Steuart Curry.

ROBERT P. CONWAY, an independent dealer and curator specializing in American prints and drawings, lives and works in Oakland, California. Formerly the Director of Associated American Artists, New York, he is now Consulting Curator to the Mills College Art Gallery, Oakland; Managing Director of the Edward Hagedorn Collection, San Francisco; and Director of the Fritz Eichenberg Trust, Peacedale, Rhode Island.

RICHARD COX is professor of art history at Louisiana State University where he lectures on American art and the history of prints. He has written at length about satirical printmaking in America, including articles and monographs on Adolf Dehn, Caroline Durieux, and Wanda Gág, among others. His article "Warrington Colescott: The London Years, 1956–66" appeared in vol. 14 of *The Tamarind Papers.*

PAT GILMOUR, who has often written for *The Tamarind Papers,* was guest editor of *TTP* 14. She served as founding curator of the print departments at the Tate Gallery, London (1974–77) and the Australian National Gallery, Canberra (1982–89); while at Canberra she edited *Lasting Impressions: Lithography as Art* (1988), a volume that included her essay "Cher Monsieur Clot: Auguste Clot and His Role as a Colour Lithographer." She is a frequent contributor to *Print Quarterly,* where her most recent articles have discussed the prints of June Wayne and R. B. Kitaj.

NANCY GREEN, Curator of Prints, Drawings, and Photographs at the Herbert F. Johnson Museum of Art, Cornell University, has written and lectured on Japonisme and its influence on the color woodcut artists of the early twentieth century. Her most recent exhibitions and catalogues are *Arthur Wesley Dow and His Influence* (1990) and *Master Prints from Upstate New York Museums* (1995). Her current projects include *Women Artists of the WPA; Temptation of the East: 100 Years of Western Printmakers in the Orient;* and a catalogue raisonné of Dow's prints.

TRUDY VICTORIA HANSEN, director of
the Morse Research Center for Graphic Arts
and curator of Prints and Drawings at the
Jane Voorhees Zimmerli Art Museum, has
held curatorial positions at the Milwaukee
Art Museum, the Chicago Historical Society,
and the Indiana University Art Museum; in
1987 she cofounded and served as associate
director of Tandem Press at the University of
Wisconsin. With cocurator Barry Walker she
has organized the current exhibition *Printmaking in America: Collaborative Prints and
Presses, 1960–1990* and coauthored its catalogue (1995).

JULIE L'ENFANT has published fiction
and criticism in the *Southern Review.* Her
novel *The Dancers of Sycamore Street* was
published by St. Martin's Press in 1983. She
is now completing a Ph.D. in art history at
the University of Minnesota with a dissertation on the art criticism of William Michael
Rossetti. In 1995 she was cocurator of an exhibition of images of women from the print
collection of the Weisman Art Museum.

JAMES WECHSLER is a painter and art
historian specializing in American art of
the 1930s and 1940s. From 1988 to 1994,
he worked for the Mary Ryan Gallery in
New York. His publications include "Fred
Becker and Atelier 17" (*Print Quarterly,*
1993) and two exhibition catalogues, *Arthur
Murphy: Prints and Drawings* and *Edward
Landon: Silkscreens* (Mary Ryan Gallery,
1993 and 1994). He is currently assisting
in an inventory of the collection at Robert
Blackburn's Printmaking Workshop in New
York and is working toward a Ph.D. degree
in art history at the CUNY Graduate Center.

GABRIEL P. WEISBERG, professor of art
history at the University of Minnesota, is an
authority on the social history of the print in
nineteenth-century France. His earlier contributions to *TTP* have included "Théophile
Steinlen and Louis Legrand: Contrasts in
Social Ideology" (1985) and "Japonisme Re-
visited: A Pioneering Exhibition Reexam-
ined" (1990). His most recent book is *The
Popularization of Images: Visual Culture
under the July Monarchy,* coedited with
Petra Ten-Doesschate Chu (1994).

PHOTO CREDITS

The Brooklyn Museum. 7.4

Christie's, New York. 7.2, 7.3

Edinburgh College of Art. 4.1

Elvehjem Museum of Art, University
   of Wisconsin, Madison. 10.1

Fine Arts Museums of San Francisco,
   Achenbach Foundation for Graphic
   Arts. 4.8

Minneapolis Institute of Arts. 2.4, 2.5;
   6.1–6.5

Musée des Beaux-Arts, Ville de Marseille.
   2.7, 2.8

National Gallery of Victoria, Melbourne.
   1.1

San Diego Museum of Art. 4.5

Tamarind Institute, University of New
   Mexico, Albuquerque. 10.2

Walker Art Center, Minneapolis.12.1, 12.2

University Art Museum, University of
   New Mexico, Albuquerque. 5.4

Worcester Art Museum, Worcester, Mass.
   5.1–5.3, 5.5–5.8; 9.2–9.10

Jane Voorhees Zimmerli Art Museum,
   New Brunswick, N.J. 3.1–3.9; 12.3, 12.4

Jack Abraham, New Brunswick, N.J. 3.1–3.9; 12.3

Will Barnet, New York. 9.1 (photographer unknown)

Charles Collier, Berkeley, Calif. 7.5, 7.6

Charles K. Cuno, Jr. 11.1, 11.2 (photographer unknown)

Wayne McCall. 4.2–4.4, 4.7

John Pachai. 4.6, 4.9

Dwight Primiano, 7.2, 7.3.

Robert C. Reck, Albuquerque. 10.2

Jack Rutberg Fine Arts, Los Angeles. 7.1

Photographs not otherwise credited, courtesy of the author of the article with which they appear.

Photo Credits